PUBLIC SPACE AND PRIVATE FAITH

A Challenge to the Churches

"If you do away with this struggle, and maintain that by tolerance, benevolence, inoffensiveness and a re-distribution or increase of purchasing power, combined with a devotion, on the part of an élite, to Art, the world will be as good as anyone could require, then you must expect human beings to become more and more vaporous."

T S Elio After Strange Gods Faber & Faber 1924

"The more individuals are promised happiness and the ideal of security, the more their unhappiness persists, the steeper the risk profile grows, and the more the victims of unkept promises revolt against those who have betrayed them."

E Roudinesco Philosophy in Turbulent Times
Columbia Univ. Press 2005

PUBLIC SPACE AND PRIVATE FAITH

A Challenge to the Churches

Alastair Redfern

ISPCK
2009

PUBLIC SPACE AND PRIVATE FAITH – Published by the Rev. Dr. Ashish Amos of the Indian Society for Promoting Christian Knowledge (ISPCK), Post Box 1585, 1654, Madarsa Road, Kashmere Gate, Delhi-110006.

ISBN: 978- 81- 8465- 033- 4

Laser typeset by **ISPCK,** Post Box 1585, 1654, Madarsa Road, Kashmere Gate, Delhi- 110006.

Tel: 23866323 / 22
e- mail– ashish@ispck.org.in • ella@ispck.org.in
website-www.ispck.org.in

CONTENTS

Preface

This essay is the fruit of a series of seminars with colleagues in the Diocese of Derby about the opportunities and challenges for the Christian Gospel in a culture which seems to encourage the privatisation of faith. Public discourse and values are increasingly rooted in an unspoken faith in secular liberal humanism – which is widely assumed to be normative for modern civilised people. This "faith" is in fact a highly sophisticated ideology, posing as both natural and neutral, presupposing individual autonomy and rights as the basis of identity, maturity and human flourishing. The drivers tend to be powerful political and economic interests and the outcome is a recipe for increasing instability and conflict.

The Gospel of Jesus Christ poses a powerful challenge to this implicit but all pervasive ideology of individual freedom. The ideas beginning to crystallise in this essay attempt to highlight the outline of an appropriate response, and the implications for Christian practice, witness and engagement. This vital and necessary task needs to be recognised and clarified to enable a more effective response to be developed. Our work in the Diocese of Derby is a small contribution to a major challenge.

This work is a development of my study of the Letter to the Hebrews "Growing the Kingdom" (ISPCK 2009). Both volumes seek to explore how we can best receive and use the gifts God provides through Jesus for advancing His Kingdom among us.

Introduction

One of the profound issues of our time is the relationship between Public Space and Private Faith. For centuries public space has been shaped by an explicit public faith, to which individuals were required to conform – sometimes actively, and sometimes by association. This public faith was proclaimed by creeds, religious organisations, representative figures and formal rituals for civic, social and personal occasions.

Since the Reformation there has been a steady shift towards an autonomous individualism[1]: from "my faith (in God) will save me" to "my faith (in myself) will guarantee my human flourishing." Religious faith has become less of a necessary framework to guide and determine the faith experience of individuals, and more of an optional resource (among many) to give confidence and comfort to individuals who choose to value those kinds of things[2].

The public realm of freedom has been created upon the basis of a new faith, a religion that takes up some of the riches of the Christian heritage, while abandoning others. This public "faith" is in the god of Toleration – offering freedom to every unique individual on their own terms (in relation to moral behaviour) and enabling a similar freedom to commercial and intellectual forces.

Regulation is provided by democracy (the will of the majority) for moral norms, and by the market for economic and political behaviour[3]. This public "faith" is not really made explicit in creeds of representative figures holding the "whole" picture. Rather, it works by being implicit – a tone rather than a formulated philosophy, thereby giving space and opportunity for its own development and unaccountability. Change and newness are the driving markers, improvement and success the key measures. One term sometimes loosely used to shorthand this universalising phenomenon is post modernism: no agreed overarching narrative, set of values or particular practices. Freedom begets freedom. The basic formation of fruitful individuals resides in Nietzsche's will to power[4].

Yet human beings exist through faith. The philosopher Hannah Arendt argued that we never know the outcome of any action or word until we act or speak because of the fact that things can go wrong, fail, be misunderstood[5]. Thus every action and word presupposes an act of faith that goodness and good outcomes are possible and worth risking.

In fact human creatures tend to explore and develop this primal "faith." Hence the history of religion and the interesting paradox that as forces of fear, terror and instability are magnified by globalising tendencies, religion has come to the fore as the key shaper not just of individual lives, but of cultural, political and moral identities. The strange exception to this trend is in Western Europe – where the work of Grace Davie has spearheaded an interesting reflection along the line of believing without belonging to organised religious groupings[6].

In Westernised countries there has been a concerted attempt to separate faith from politics[7]. "Religious" faith is a private matter: politics is the organised worship of the god of Toleration, under the guise of democracy (involving the free will of every individual). Such a distinction is developing on other continents too. Religious groups are tempted to cooperate with this separation since it creates a comfortable space for pastoral performance around the inevitable needs and sufferings of human beings, while removing any responsibility for prophetic interpretation and action that would challenge the uncritical worship of the god of Toleration. In fact much modern theology has been conveniently recast to support this ideology, with priority given to inclusion, variety, and the positiveness of difference – the theology of the Trinity has been especially emphasised to provide a superficial endorsement for the values of diversity in unity and the importance of community[8].

Christian theology is public theology. It proclaims a common and focussing faith in One God: One Lord: One Church. The kingdom of God is an all embracing call to humanity in all its variety and brokenness to find a common connection and salvation in a Creator God made manifest in Jesus Christ, and issuing as energy and gift in a Spirit of Holiness. Christian theology is not primarily pastoral: the outpouring of love is a gift which follows the repentance of turning away from self and selfishness to give priority to God's universalising agenda of kingdom. Such faith is the "elemental energy of the soul."[9], an intuition deep in human hearts for connection and communion with others, with creation, with the Creator. This faith can never be "private" or limited to demonstrations of care: it provides a lens and an agenda through which life can risk to be lived – even via failure and death; because the core is a focus on eternity and a totally different, corporate kind of fulfilment.

This essay explores the tensions between public space, the privatisation of faith, and the challenge to reconnect them. It suggests a casting down of the god of Toleration, to create space for giving proper weight to the negative aspects of human being, as a way of freeing more fruitful forces of creativity.

CHAPTER I

The Shape of Public Space

The Church of England has employed a number of ways of giving shape to public space so that Christian faith provides the key element. Each has been undermined by the inexorable shift from corporate to individual identities.

From the Reformation the basic tool was the Book of Common Prayer. This provided a theological framework for public worship in every community, and for the key moments of human being: birth, marriage, sickness, serious sin, death. The uniformity of language and basic practice enable the "faith" of individuals to be formed and framed in a common container, giving powerful witness to One Lord, one faith, one church, one civil society. Reality was clearly corporate.

More recently, liturgy has moved from a comprehensive book of common prayer, with fixed forms and formulae, to a notion of common worship – with a basic structure, but a plethora of choices to suit particular people and contexts. There is little sense of common prayer in the contemporary Church of England: more the problem of finding connection and coherence between a multitude of localised practices and preferences. The focus is increasingly found not in any sense of public liturgy, but in the performance of the particular priest and president of that congregation. Worship provides a localised common place for those who attend, but offers little that is a recognisable public faith to those outside in the wider community.

The theology and the practice varies enormously, and traditional structures such as the Diocese or Deanery are being replaced for many practical purposes of identity and connection with more specific webs of relationships such as Forward in Faith, Reform, Inclusive Church, Affirming Catholicism, or the Evangelical Alliance. The notion of "public" faith has been abandoned. Faith is held in private gatherings and networks, and then offered in the spiritual market place as an invitation to others. The result is an intensification of emphasis upon the Christian Gospel as something for individuals to choose to join through particularised groups, offering worship as affirmation and formation within that context - doing good in a needy world (as personal witness and invitation) and abandoning the wider issues of political, economic, cultural values and visions. In this sense the shifting conglomerates of private faith groups and individuals who join with others to enflesh the reality of toleration is the only way in which to handle public space. The call of the creator God to be stewards of the whole of creation is relegated to a pious aspiration.

An interesting indicator of this shift is the growth of a new kind of Marcionism: reading scripture selectively to concentrate upon the wholesome parts which witness to love and community, and ignoring the political agendas and those calling for sacrifice, suffering and sojourning in the wilderness.

This mirrors developments in the political world, whereby differences are handled through the building of relationships between those holding different views, as a foundation from which new perspectives might emerge, but primarily as a means of emphasising coexistence and the postponement of engaging decisively with rival and incompatible views and values. This "road map" approach has much to commend it, as the recent history of Northern Ireland makes clear. It is a method deliberately adopted at the 2008 Lambeth Conference – with a determination not to make decisions, but to build fellowship among disciples of Jesus Christ[1].

But the approach has dangers – not least the implication that incompatible views are of secondary importance: human flourishing on anyone's own chosen terms and toleration are the key. This theology owes more to Hegel than to Jesus, Paul, Augustine or any of the foundational figures of the faith[2]. Communion is not simply about participation, which seems to be the way in which contemporary Christianity is tempted to handle difference. Rather, holy communion is about repentance, purification, one Lord and a coherent life in Him.

As liturgical resources for providing common ground have unravelled, synodical government has offered a religious version of the nineteenth century's approach to diversity – not common values but an all embracing bureaucracy. Rules and regulations hold the ring for common life, other values are merely personal and private. This is the technique which has given space for the capitalist and sexual revolutions to explode, isolating individuals as consumers and postponing points of solid connection and mutual accountability indefinitely[3]. A "temporary" bureaucracy holds the ring and in fact under the guise of freedom the ruling powers are self satisfaction, abuse, oppression and marginalisation. Hence the growth in pornography, sex trafficking, global poverty, inequality within nations, psychological disorders. Atomisation leads to anomie – but the next election or improved product hold out the promise of salvation.

This way of procedure through atomisation is reflected in contemporary politics. As political parties have collapsed, and modern media becomes so pervasive, there has been a steady development of "sofa government." Leaders sit on the sofa in a television studio, interviewed by a carefully chosen, benign interviewer! The result is a new genre of Messiahship. The "leader" speaks to each person directly in their own private space, promising to solve all problems and provide the conditions for human flourishing. Knowing the sheer variety of hopes and values within a state, the Messiah can only connect positively by appealing to selfishness (lower taxes: less constraints on personal freedoms, invitations to comment on or take charge of public services) and thus to the god of Toleration. In reality, viewers are completely disempowered, as are other people in that political party. There is a direct transaction between leader and led: undeliverable promises are made, and are attractive because they are truly "miraculous."

In the same way, churches are increasingly searching for "Messiah leadership": strong, directional, but giving an impression of meaningful participation. The result is priority for a "sofa" atmosphere, some tough rhetoric, but no means to deliver meaningful change either in the lifestyles of participants or in that of the wider community. Faith remains privatised and public space dominated by the god of Toleration. Church membership operates through choice and market forces. In seeking political or religious leaders there is an emphasis upon effective management and good relationships. Very little emphasis is given to the dark elements of life: sin, suffering, the call to change and to sacrifice self for the sake of a greater whole. Not only does this contradict the public dimension of Christian faith, but it contains the seeds of destruction for a civilisation built upon the god of Toleration and the method of democracy. Individual liberalism defies effective management because rights are not easily made compatible, and the more emphasis given to "toleration", the more resentment tends to result if the will of the majority is seen to prohibit or undermine the values and "rights" of others. This incompatibility provides the seedbed of conflict at many levels across the globe, and is a major reason for the attractiveness of fundamentalisms and force: rights need protection, and the god of Toleration is always found wanting once the first stages of relationship building has been explored.

The twin issues for human living are those of authority (who decides, and on what grounds) and the means of creative coexistence. Each needs the other, and one of the problems of contemporary approaches is the tendency to separate them into political and social/economic areas. The traditional word for handling both of these issues is "sovereignty." Who rules? – God, myself, the church, the state, or commercial forces – today the list is endless. Sovereignty is always contested and complex: but the degrees of complexity and competition to "rule" have increased dramatically.

Sovereignty is a key theological concept. The sign is that of a throne – evident in scripture and presupposed as fundamental in the teaching of Jesus about a king and a kingdom. In early religious cultures sovereignty was dispersed and localised - the theology of Baal. Different gods for different places and activities. Israel bore witness to one God – one sovereign Lord, but her history is an account of dispersal and localisation, through compromise with neighbouring religions and through a variety of emphases within her own belief systems. The Roman Imperium operated a similar mixed economy: the cult of the Emperor was officially supreme, but in fact local sovereignties were permitted. In each of these ecologies sovereignty tended to be focussed in a key person and was held to be absolute, and yet in practice it operated within the limitations of the particular context – the olive grove, the family, Israel. In this way sovereignty provided both an overarching source of law and authority, and yet the space for a more localised manifestation, enabling differences and variety to be held together creatively.

Even within the mediaeval Christendom system, there were tensions between ecclesial and political sovereignties, both in their overarching claims and in their localised operation. This potential for fragmentation was realised in the Reformation: though each "part" often espoused a universal and absolute aspiration. Thus there developed an underlying contestedness and complexity – which has been increasingly illustrated by a de facto handling through implicit recognition of the supremacy of Toleration, and yet a covert desire for conversion or conquest of those who differ. This is true for both religious and political entities. Concepts such as international law seek to provide a framework of sovereignty, but beneath the surfaces these deeper contradictory currents remain powerful[4]. Institutions and individuals steadily claim more rights for themselves, as sovereignty becomes more self-consciously focussed around particular views and values. The best example is the tyranny of liberalism, so frequently expressed by those who demand that people with more circumscribed frameworks for living and relating should be more "open" and "inclusive." The liberalism that worships the god of Toleration tries to unite support by undermining more closed and compacted approaches but in fact contains a myriad of competing and incompatible claims to sovereignty – exposed around issues such as abortion, euthanasia, prostitution, property and abuse of self and others.

Thus there are competing claims to sit on the throne: universal religions, nation states, individuals – each making an absolute claim. Messiahship is an obvious method of trying to "transcend" these claims through a representative person who promises fulfilment to all. By contrast Jesus promised a way of the cross, and a fulfilment in eternity: a teleological take on Messiahship totally absent from a secular world obsessed with measuring results and setting performance targets. Moreover the fleeting "contact" between sofa Messiahs and the people they claim to save means that much happens through inertia. Promises are rarely seen through – they are simply re-packaged and changed. On an issue such as abortion, what began as a concession to the will of the majority has subtly shifted into something much more normative in everyday life with no proper discussion or accountability for leaders exercising sovereignty. Such "hot potatoes" are passed to a "free vote": the ultimate sovereignty – with no direction about the big picture or a range of alternatives from those actually pulling the strings.

In this instance, faith is a private resource for individuals, but has no sovereign status in decision making processes. Yet the "faith" of those individuals, if it is Christian, claims an absolute sovereignty on moral issues – not always in terms of clarity of decision-making, which often needs time for discernment but with regard to the factors needing to be part of any evaluative discussion: for example the sanctity of life, and the fact that the "individual" does not exist in Christian theology, only persons-in-relationship, with God and with others.

People of Faith are called to abandon the sovereignty of God, and any sense of a divinely governed moral order. God is reduced to being a resource for individuals, the ultimate Faith is in Hegelian dialectic to tease out synthesis and connection between differences, the sovereignty of the majority (based on a faith-less public discourse and debate) and the priority of toleration to maintain "peace and unity." Any higher, more demanding and possibly more life changing claim is excluded from public space. Christians conform by majoring on theologies of mission by example and withdrawn integrity within a private space.

This challenge is highlighted in Holy Week, when Jesus chooses a donkey to be His throne – moving to a cross five days later. This is a very different sign of sovereignty in human form: humble, inconclusive in terms of the promises of sofa Messiahs, but touching deeper chords in human hearts. Purification and self abnegation provide a different currency of Sovereignty, one through which leaders and their followers can be joined together, rooted in realism about darkness, death, lack, longing – rather than simple concentration upon artificial illumination, privileged life, plenty and satisfaction. The first provides the ingredients of a genuine spirituality, the second offers narcissistic nihilism.

The fact that government is concerned about social cohesion is testament to the way in which dispersed and localised sovereignty, overseen by sofa Messiahship, is leading. British citizenship ceremonies take us back to the Roman Imperium; citizenship is the key to cohesion, accessed through a minimalist public ritual and allegiance to the tolerant state. The total failure to engage with the harsh social and political realities which have hitherto prevented people properly belonging, and still exclude many more from effective citizenship, is illustrative of the gap between the bourgeois rhetoric of individual autonomy, and the sovereignty of the state through the exercise of sofa Messiahship on the one hand, and the cries of human hearts for something richer on the other.

The obfuscation of these realities is provided by a combination of the forces of fashion, always encouraging people to seek newer identities, with the marks being provided by capitalism's latest, carefully targeted, offerings; and the ever new promises of greater perfection through the sovereignty of the sofa and the state. People put their faith in these twin forces, and any other ingredients have to be confined to the private sphere of consenting adults in particularised places.

When churches offer more public rituals and pronouncements they are almost always within the framework of a capitalistic emphasis upon the precious uniqueness of each person and the beckoning of perfect community that politicians and the pressure groups who own and control modern societies prescribe .

A public faith promotes a man sat on a donkey, and then hung from a cross, as a warning about sovereignty and an invitation to a very different kind of citizenship. Jesus said "only one is good" (Luke 18^{19}). The tendency of human systems of sovereignty is to promote what is good. For Christians, only One is good. We are called to be what psychoanalysts would sometimes call "good enough," set free from sin but knowing that sin remains. The sovereignty of the One who is good, frees up His children to be good enough – purified and infused by grace through trusting in His call and His kingdom, but realistic about failure, incompletion, ragged edges. As a result the aim is not for the perfections of sofa Messiahship, but for the realities of frail fleshliness and hopeful human hearts. This is the key middle territory obscured by a culture of rights, individual and state sovereignty managed by promises of miracles that can never deliver the good, or even the good enough. The Christian task is to chart this territory and claim a prior sovereignty that puts all else in its place.

CHAPTER 2

Embracing Sovereignty
with Integrity

Sovereignty is usually expressed through law, sometimes through ritual. Law creates the obligation and guidance which enables conformity to the rule being exercised. Sovereigns normally have "subjects," those formed by the rule being exercised.

Political law depends ultimately upon force – sometimes military, sometimes in terms of the will of the majority in a democracy. Jesus was content to live under Roman political law. Render to Caesar (Luke 20[25]) was recognition of the necessity of this kind of sovereignty, as was a willingness to pay taxes, even if the money was raised in an unconventional way! (Matthew 17[24-27]).

A different kind of sovereignty is exercised by religious law, which depends upon commitment, though sometimes underscored by force. An experience of grace induces a desire to conform to certain beliefs and behaviours: in New Testament times about diet, divorce, marriage, worship (Matthew 5-7). Christendom tried to combine political and religious law, and discovered that this neat coupling was impossible, because law that depends upon force, either physical or as expressed by the will of the majority, is fundamentally different from law that depends upon commitment.

Both of these types of sovereignty, political and religious, operate through a direct dynamic between those who exercise such authority, and those who are formed and disciplined to conform accordingly.

In the Christian Gospel we meet a third kind of law, the law of love. (John 15$^{12\text{-}13}$). It comes out of encounter - with a person, a place, an incident – through which the heart is opened, and greater possibilities begin to be grasped. Often such encounter is with elements of glory and grace, or with elements of darkness and danger: both the glory of the mountain top and the terror of the wilderness can be sites of such engagement. Jesus on the mount of transfiguration, or on the cross, Paul healing a sick person or on the road to Damascus. This kind of encounter opens the heart to new things, often at cost to what has been. It provides a template for understanding law and sovereignty, and the role of subjects and citizens. When these moments of encounter occur they need to be examined and explored, by the recipient and with others – family, group or tribe; various kinds of associations within which the individual person can acknowledge and investigate larger possibilities.

In the case of Jesus, He works out His experience of God's grace in His baptism and call, and His ongoing encounters with others, by sharing with a group of three (Peter, James, John) with a group of twelve, with a group of seventy-two and with a group of women who were part of His ministry. Similarly Paul used Timothy and others such as Apollos. He has Elders in each city, and also local church groups. There is a variety of contexts within which the experience of encounter is put alongside that of others, in small groupings, to be refined, challenged and clarified. These forums provide a safe and creative space to consider the discourse of the heart in relation to others, and in relation to the overall political and religious systems of sovereignty. The "rule" being offered is tested alongside a more personal tasting of life and the moments that seem to matter in terms of illumination, expectation and purification.

Jesus constantly places these refining encounters within the context of a single, universal kingdom. Paul writes letters to draw the experience of local association into the catholicity of the one church. The concentrated and tested experience of individuals and small groupings needs to be brought into the common currency of language, theology and practice.

Between a personal, individual sense of identity and the absolute, universalising claims of sovereignty of state and/or religion, come these key sites of formation and deepening, providing both critique and confirmation of what might be on offer – from within and from without: These are encounters of the heart. There needs to be an interplay between political law (enforcing conformity), religious law (inviting commitment) and the formation-of-the-person-through-intimate-relationships (exploring and evaluating conformity and commitment).

The danger of sofa Messiahship and the twin forces of globalisation and localisation /individualism is that sovereignty is understood simply as a transaction between the central/universal and the particular person/locality. Thus the political rule of law is exercised by the will of the majority: everyone must conform. The religious rule of a Faith is exercised by its traditional teachings, or increasingly in the West, through the will of majorities in synodical processes. What is missing is the space for sovereignty to be explored and evaluated in the key groups through which human beings are formed. Between the individual and the institution are a myriad of key sites for real encounter (heart speaking to human heart) whereby perspective and commitment can be enhanced. Instead of seeking immediate response to issues in terms of the will of the majority at a macro level, there needs to be space to investigate sovereignty which can be appropriated, developed or challenged by more than a simple assent or dissent. The lack of such space for appropriation, exploration and creative critique explains the deep cynicism in western politics. The only serious players seem to be the state (ruled by sofa Messiahship) and the individual receiver in front of their screen. The scope for real connection is crude, over simplistic and unlikely to satisfy the personal demand for rights and autonomy. Many faith organisations are being tempted to use technology and communications resources to inculcate a parallel dynamic between the sovereignty of the message being proclaimed and the commitment of the receiver. Thus theology, liturgical practice, and moral behaviours become ever more simplistic, crude and unable to produce deep transformation. Much popular expression of faith is constantly undermined by outbreaks of cynical self-righteousness, over quick judgements and defensive, inward looking strategies.

Between the big picture with its overarching principles and ultimate sovereignty and the micro seeking for meaning, direction and personal sovereignty lies the rich territory within which most human being unfolds: small, shifting formational groups. J. N. Figgis, an Anglican divine in the early twentieth century called them "associations."[1] His contemporary William Temple spoke of mediating principles[2].

By associations Figgis meant family, school, workplace, town, country, church: in each place there is an opportunity for real engagement with the encounters of the heart. These include encounters with the claims of political and religious sovereignty, but placing these in a much broader and more realistic context – that of engagement which forms the individual within a web of relationships loaded with potential meaning, and intimate enough to bear interpretation that can be experienced as both realistic and hopeful of much beyond. Political and religious sovereignty can only operate by embracing this inevitable work of the heart – reflective, emotional, intellectual and deeply intuitive. Individuals can only exercise any kind of personal sovereignty if their relationship with the holders of the bigger picture is properly mediated through this middle territory: each of these "associations" has an independent life and an interdependent life. None of them is a site of sovereignty as claimed by institutions or individuals, but without them sovereignty can never be more than a law which will breed cynicism and revolt alongside conformity. The distinctive yet changing identity of each "association" allows for change, development and pruning – a negotiation of sovereignty into everyday life. There is engagement with failure as well as success.

This model has been a key element of traditional Anglicanism. Between the Bishop representing the fullness of the church, and the parochialism of her local expressions there have been mediating spaces for comparing independent testimonies, enabling exploration and negotiation. The thirty-nine Articles recognise the key roles of Councils and of the local congregation, but somewhere in between are the mechanisms by which the cure of souls is shared and a complex of checks and balances ensures space for reflection, testing and tasting. There is a danger that the predominance of a General (National) Synod is sweeping away all these precious intermediate spaces of formation and reproducing a political system that seeks direct transaction between the centre and the separated individual or localised context.

Kingdoms and Body are both complex biblical images of a redeemed people whose life depends upon the internal workings and the particular contribution of those elements that connect the whole with the various parts.

Formation through such intermediate associations will never be "good" in a pure sense, but it can be "good enough." This enables the initiative to remain dependent upon the gift of grace, yet robust enough to produce real results. Moreover the model of association makes clear the necessity of receiving from others. Like an individual, no small group or association can survive on its own. Besides requiring its own space for meaningful encounter, each association needs to develop ways of engaging with others – thus encounter becomes a way of evaluating, expressing and enhancing individuals-in-relationship: a model which is deeply opposed to rule by sofa Messiahship.

Figgis argued that the state is "a society of societies" and that loyalties to the state need to be based on these prior loyalties to the constitutive associations. In this sense humans are social beings, before they are political beings. The unit of civil life is not the individual but the family i.e. the individual in relationship[3].

Sovereignty needs macro and micro expression – but it is in the medium space that key work is achieved to enable fruitful but not uncritical participation. Human being lies in the individual, the association, and the corporate. As family life and stable associations dissolve this is a challenging agenda – illustrated by David Putnam's famous analysis Bowling Alone[4] - charting the shift within this popular activity from a team and group basis to one of individual participation and performance.

The image of a man on a donkey surrounded by groups of followers is a sign of sovereignty that can be explored through networks of associations. We need to give priority to these sites of formation and spiritual transaction as key to both individual and corporate identity.

For local churches this implies a challenge to move from beyond the network of groups which comprise a church (congregations, choir, toddlers, lunch club etc) to serious engagement with the associations under such pressure from a culture of direct transaction between sofa Messiahship and individual being – the google world of direct connection between the person and the answer. This middle territory of groups and associations is the place where the agenda of the heart can be encountered, illuminated, challenged and changed. The Sovereign Lord exercises sovereignty in the church, through the state, in individual lives – but also in the associations which frame and interpret the encounters of the heart. Spaces where exploration takes precedence over ready answers, so that goodness can be handled with hope rather than triumphal, excluding arrogance or cynical, resigned rejection. The Word requires words – interpretation around our real experiences and encounters, in all their hopefulness and imperfection. Places for encounters that are always partial, too small and yet the germ of greater aspiration. Jesus' whole style is about reflection, engagement, exploration of moreness – alongside a sovereignty of clear traditions and practices to help shape formation that can transform sinners and fill people with hope. The task of the church is to enable what Anglican Divines in the sixteenth century called "sound learning" – accepting the sovereignty of God through church and state, through every creature, and through the intermediate associations where the implications and possibilities can best be recognised and received.

A public faith will provide interpretation between different communities of formation, offering sound learning and foundational moments to enable interpretation of encounters experienced by individuals, and thus to help provide suitable material for the ongoing construction of the biggest picture. Anglicanism has a long tradition of operating in these spaces within local and civic communities, offering light and leaven which flows from the parallel discipline of gathered worship and more overtly theological reflection.[5] A major challenge of our time is to maintain and develop the dynamic between a gathered group and the opportunities for wider encounter and association.

CHAPTER 3

Environmental Choices

Public space exists in a number of different environments, each providing a context for private faith to find direction and possible fulfilment.

The basic environment is that of the physical creation, explored in the early chapters of Genesis. This is the territory of the human body and the eco systems within which it exists. The Green agenda calls private faith to be joined to a more public concern for the proper stewardship of the body, of humankind and of the environment. Response to natural disasters illustrates how human hearts react to those encounters with vulnerability and mortality in a corporate and caring manner.

However, human beings have the capacity to create a second environment[1], as exemplified in Acts 17 where Paul debates with Greek philosophers on the Areopagus. This is the creation of a world of ideas and images, hopes and values – the cultivation of civilisation. This second environment transcends human mortality and the limitations of the physical environment – just as the vision of angels at the birth of Jesus provided a larger canopy within which to understand this infant and His potentiality. Such signs and concepts give significance and shape to human existence, but as Genesis Chapter 3 illustrates, human knowledge operates through the making of choices, some of which are good and some of which are evil. This work of discernment both unites (Adam and Eve shared the apple) and yet divides (they begin arguing about who was responsible for that course of action). In this narrative the physicality of the created environment quite literally provides food for further thought and a new kind of creation – the cultivation of civilisation.

Psychology has shown how human beings can construct a private second environment, but these "new worlds" need testing with others and at numerous levels, from the most intimate, through groups and associations, to identity within broader political and cultural contexts. Beyond the physical and the instinctual, there is the world of wonder, imagination, value, fear, ultimacy, eternity, divinity.

Just as the primary environment operates through the paradoxes of complementarity and conflict, so the construction of this second environment is subject to the same forces. Thus there is a tendency to trust (have faith in) the cosiness of manageable communities, or simply in the self-as-community in a world which seems ever more fragile and unable to provide the stability and support each person craves. The result is a cocktail of shifting tribalism and defensive selfishness. Each element is constructed around a limited yet apparently manageable second environment. Yet, deep in human hearts is the capacity to imagine and desire greater things – universal, eternal – the stuff of catholicity. The task of the church is to engage with these different levels of creating a spiritual environment, and to call people, through word and example (sacrament) to trust in more ultimate possibilities.

In civic society such faith has been given public focus at different levels. For example the Greeks valued the oikos or household, the polis or city as a collection of households, and eventually empire as a conglomerate of cities. A similar dynamic is evident in Jewish culture, with the family being the base unit for worship and identity, finding local focus in the synagogue, and a more universal expression in the Temple. Jesus inhabited these kinds of ecology, and offered a similar scheme – the small groups which He gathered around Him, the chosen people to be light and leaven, and the light for the world which embraced gentiles of every hue.

In each setting the environment is created through the interplay of tradition, current experience, and challenging signs. Often private faith was nourished in quite specific moments ("your faith has saved you"), but always within the context of a call and challenge to experience something more embracing and universal in potential. Private faith is called out of the self to be joined in richer aspirations that transcend limitations and localness through the energy of a common hope – one which can inspire individual members to make sacrifice on behalf of this more glorious construction and possibility. These processes operate through dialogue and debate as choices are discerned and responses crafted. The dynamic of being united and divided is a continuing feature. An example would be the gathering around Jesus to hear a parable and then the variety of interpretations and appropriations. This is why a history and liturgical practice held in common are important, not least in helping to provide a holding environment for the ceaseless movement of union and fraction by which communion in pursued and received.

Thus revelation, the new seeing of faith, emerges from the sacrifice of self and a purely private perception, and from trusting engagement with the robust but ultimately rewarding processes of finding faith with others in a public space that is continually under construction, and changing through growth and pruning as the processes of uniting and dividing continue. Christians recognise this dynamic as atonement: Jesus said "If I be lifted up, I will draw all people to myself." (John 12[32]). The brokenness of crucifixion of the self is the sign of sacrifice that enables a more public manifestation of faith in goodness and glory emerging from death and destruction. This spirituality of sacrificing certainties for God's greater possibilities is the root of our human capacity to give ourselves away in love for others, and to embrace bigger perspectives than our own experience might deem feasible. In this sense Jesus becomes the new Temple, place of ultimacy and eternity providing a model of public faith which can embrace all private beliefs and behaviour. Public space is created by atonement – the giving of the private and limited to the greater purposes of God.

But there are particular ways of proceeding which become clear through the way in which Jesus orders ministry for this essential mission – the salvation of humankind through our capacity for creativity and change. Jesus begins with the bedrock of private faith. He calls, challenges and commissions individuals. Yet personal faith in Jesus is faith in "Our Father", an energy of the soul which seeks greater connection and fulfilment. And because this private faith has to be expressed and explored in such a public arena (of other disciples and of God's saving call to creation) the sheer variety of those who respond results in continuing debate and dialogue among the disciples, and between them and those as yet on the outside of their working together to help create the second environment through which salvation can be given: the arena of spiritual life. The dynamic of uniting in a common life and yet dividing over interpretation and strategies is at the heart of the public space being created: the formation of God's "second environment."

This is particularly noteworthy given the context within which Jesus was operating, shaped by two contrasting forces for creating and managing public space. The predominant model was that of the Roman Empire with its notion of citizenship, a core allegiance to the Empire, and the toleration of a whole variety of local constructions of public space – a policy which provided valuable space for the Jewish nation at that time. This pattern parallels some of the main strategies in western liberal democratic society: a legal, bureaucratic framework for citizenship in terms of political loyalty, and toleration of a wide variety of belief and behaviour in local contexts. The main aim is to maintain peace and prevent people damaging each other. Thus public space is a tiered second environment: an overarching political system based upon force, and a plethora of more local constructions, free to pursue their own plans, within this overall holding mechanism. Religion is confined to the "private" and small scale enterprises. Public faith is in the ultimacy of the system and its current "Messiah" operators: this is the focus of worth-ship in terms of seeking security and stability, a secular form of salvation from the vagaries and destructive tendencies of human beings.

Besides this Roman model there was also present in the time of Jesus and Paul a Greek approach – based upon a diversity of ideas, open to debate and discovery ("Sir, we would see Jesus." John 12[20]). This was the method of the Areopagus (Acts 17[22]), where competitive debate aimed to win support and there was an underlying hermeneutic of suspicion in terms of faith in anything fixed or enduring being constructed. The sheer drama of life was best investigated through narrative, poetry and philosophical speculation – seeds of what today might be termed post modernism. Freedom is the key: form will follow.

Amidst these competing models of how best to construct public space, the people of God had retreated into self-referencing groups: private strongholds of a faith held narrowly and defensively – Pharisees, Sadducees, Zealots, Essenes. This approach is always a powerful temptation, since the smaller the scale of construction, the more certainty seems to be possible, with stability and security under closer control. Throughout the history of the church, including strategies in our own times, this retreat into apparently secure, clear spaces with strong boundaries has been a powerful pattern for handling the impulse of the spiritual life. The key is self sacrifice to the system as constructed, rather than to a process expecting new and greater possibilities. This pattern reflected that of the Roman Empire, implying the ultimacy of the god of Toleration, but obscuring this reality by a fierce focus upon a small self-referencing world of defensive construction, within which the piercing openness of Jesus' teaching and example have a very limited role.

By contrast, in the New Testament we see Jesus call people to break open these small boxes, and model an open, porous, shifting community seeking always to see more clearly the ultimate purposes of God. Hence construction of a public, second environment will involve the fraction of pruning alongside the tasting of unity.

The method of Jesus is to call two core groups who are very close to Him and who argue, debate and learn, often through making mistakes. They argue about money, goodness, theories of leadership, the person of Jesus and Peter's confession. One of the core groups is Peter, James and John. The second core group is made up of women, Mary, Joanna and others. These two core groups are complemented by the twelve. Each unit is a place of diversity, difference and dialogue, yet committed to seeing what is not yet seen. These are the ingredients for continuing His sacred mission of constructing the environment of salvation. Each group is self-consciously an agent of engagement with the Divine call to kingdom, manifest in Jesus Himself, and with all kinds of others – as individuals, in groups, as nations. The synagogue provides a bedrock for local rooting in scripture, tradition and public worship. Similarly, Paul develops dogma, disciplines and ministerial structures. The Temple provides a universal focus for the mystery of sacrifice of self to enable God's greater gift of new life to be received. In Christian liturgy the Temple becomes the Body of Christ.

With these groups (associations connecting to other associations) and with these resources for local and universal worship, Jesus engages with the current ways of constructing a second environment. He does not try to overthrow either the Roman or the Greek systems: He pays His taxes and He engages with Greek seekers. Human beings will always need to construct public space through political organisation and philosophic exploration. Jesus offers no blueprint to supersede either approach.

Rather, He trains His small associations to engage with each method of construction at the points where there is a gap between the public space they are being invited to inhabit and the actual hopes and hurts in human hearts. There will always be a gap in human lives, such is the power of faith and hope: this is the arena of the spiritual life: Public space constructed by politics and by philosophy can never provide ultimate healing and wholeness.

Similarly Jesus accepts the self-referencing groups into which the people of God had retreated. He challenges them to be more open to the potential creativity of grace and forgiveness, but He accepts that there needs to be an element of more localised "association" alongside a faith in greater public possibilities.

The key to this engagement with the political, philosophic and religious constructions of public space is prayerful reflectiveness. Where hurt and hope remain unsatisfied, there needs to be further dialogue and discovery, seeking more connection with the catholicity of "Our (common) Father" and His all embracing kingdom of salvation. The results will never be the emergence of perfection in the human performance of politics, philosophy or religion: rather the outcome will be more confidence in the deeper intuition of the heart that such constructs are always limited, penultimate and lacking in fullness. Hurt and hope continue in human hearts as the currency of an aspiration that needs to be explored in a dynamic between the fraction that owns and explores the imperfection of every human construct, while recognising that this necessary reality can be embraced by the deeper discourse of giving up the self's search for security and stability, and trusting that such sacrifice in fact opens up a stream of new life that handles hurt and hope in the context of eternity. There will be moments of grace and encouragement, calls to change and try new constructions, but always at the altar of sacrifice. Signs and rituals, parables and prayers, are the resources the small associations offer as seeds of salvation to others.

This shift of perspective is sometimes summarised in terms of owning the necessary but limited importance of interdependence: careful construction of catholicity according to canons of measurement and performance. Of more significance is the spiritual notion of interpenetration – a deeper, hidden connectivity with God and with each other, through the more limited constructs of politics, philosophy and formal religion. Hence the priority of prayer to own hurt and hope in the human heart, and reflect before God as to how these realities can challenge and change the creation of public space in a way that should involve each person as a participant, but not necessarily produce immediately compelling outcomes.

The task of those called to discipleship is to give priority to this prayerful reflection, and to be open to changes in the structures we are called to build as containers for political, cultural and religious living.

Given the tendency in western culture to privatise faith, and to organise public space on the basis of efficiency and maximum toleration of difference, the task of the church and her ministry is both daunting and yet vital if the cycle of cynicism and nihilism is to be broken apart, not least so that the hurts and hopes of millions of the earth's inhabitants can be part of the prayerful reflection about constructing a second environment and with a genuine ultimacy of purpose.

There will always be a tension between the value of comfortable communities – because that is what human beings need in terms of shelter and stability – and the deeper spiritual engagement of prophecy and an ever greater catholicity of fellowship, both of which are continually critiquing and shaping the construction of public space.

CHAPTER 4

The Art of Association

In the ministry of Jesus there are two distinct yet complementary patterns that fashion the art of association – for particular groups and for their interaction. Both reflect a dynamic operating within the Jewish tradition, as illustrated through Moses and Ezra, and evident in the early church, especially in the Acts of the Apostles.

The first impetus is outward. It is mirrored by Paul and the history of Christian mission. The Gospel is so powerful and precious that it brings good news to every creature. There is an urgency to encounter and invite everyone. Traditional barriers and boundaries have to be transgressed: seed is scattered wherever Jesus and the apostles journey. As a result, all kinds of people respond and want to engage with Jesus and the Gospel of a kingdom of love and new life. Jesus is restless, always keen to move on to the next village, nervous of simply settling down around signs of success to embroider a still greater security. Faith is about movement into other areas of public space, like light and leaven transforming all who come into contact with such a powerful force. Jesus is seen as the Son of Man – representative of everyone.

Of course such reckless transgressing of the normal boundaries of association causes problems too. The simple message of God's love, forgiveness and salvation becomes ever more complex because each person or group appropriates their particular encounter in a different way – misunderstandings and competing claims arise: much seems unfinished, tantalising but still lacking. As a result, Jesus begins to develop a complementary strategy. Alongside the outward flow of teaching, healing, challenging – He creates an inward momentum, calling small groups together to be deepened in the fundamentals, and to become guides and arbiters of the missionary endeavours. The bewildering variety of encounters and aspirations needs a "rock" of solid words and signs – a church as Peter and Paul were to learn together in the Acts of the Apostles. The pure essence will need to risk serious dilution by being poured out so freely: the fruits need a reference point for subsequent reflection and refinement. The task of apostleship is to oversee these complementary movements of risky, generous, indiscriminate outflow and the maintenance of a core measure and guide which is clearly focussed upon the Word and Sacraments specifically provided by God in remembrance of Him. In this part of the narrative Jesus is more often referred to as the "Son of God." In this way the church is called upon to act as a particularly complex association, offering both styles of engagement to other groups whose faith and style will tend to be more particular and limited in terms of the contrasting models outlined above. This requires faith in a complex construction of public space – that second more spiritual environment – trusting in the value of both freedom and focus: the Gospel invites participation of all people, on their own terms, and on the specific terms provided in Jesus Christ.

In practice this means that the church will run a mixed economy: open associations such as mums and toddlers, Harvest celebrations or Alpha Courses: and focussed core groups rooted in word, sacrament and the discipline of prayerful reflection. This double task is the work of discipleship – operating in both kinds of public space, and seeking to make creative connections between them.

The same dynamic needs to flow within acts of public worship. There is a formal framework and key ingredients that are important to core participants. Many others, including regular worshippers, simply need space to engage within a particular service in ways that give meaning to them at that moment. There is no attempt to appreciate or access the "whole" – just a trust that on any one occasion, something in the atmosphere or the ingredients will be helpful and enriching. Some people will only attend for a particular occasion, and will be engaged in a very specific way – for instance if grandchildren are in a parade service for uniformed organisations.

On such complex occasions, public worship acts as a resource to a whole variety of private faith needs, and a wide range of endeavours to construct more public spaces within which a fuller life might unfold. The formal ingredients of word and sacrament are crucial, because people can be freed to dip in and out of the liturgy in ways that help them most. There is coherence in overall elements such as attendance and aspiration, but incoherence in the cultivation of faith and action. This reality provides an important context for understanding the working of private faith, particular associations, and the dynamics which recognise their existence per se, while inviting an ever broader engagement – recognising the need for retrenchment and focus too. The art of association is in offering such opportunities and dynamics.

The classical approach to discerning truth, which involves constructing a pattern to give meaning to experience and ideas, is thus challenged by the need to recognise as equally important the role of process. How patterns are constructed, critiqued and sometimes changed is something explored through taking seriously the dynamics and creating of association. For Christians there is a pattern provided in Jesus Christ: Son of Man and Son of God. This pattern is discerned, proclaimed, performed and purified by a process through which its enfleshment in the public space is constantly monitored, reflected upon and infused with richer insights through the spirit of holiness and wholeness. The temptation for every Christian grouping or association is to solidify its experience of God's grace by boundaries of belief and behaviour, creating barriers with other associations outside, and implying that pure faith is a private possession. The outgoing impetus of the ministry of Jesus and Paul stands as a permanent challenge to this tendency, and invites a richer understanding of the art of association and the creation of a spiritual environment as public space.

Two theological tools can resource this responsibility. The first is the notion of hierarchy. Jesus is Lord. Hierarchy does not simply mean "raised up over others" or "superior." It means appointed to represent the whole – which is always superior to the parts. In this sense Jesus commissioned apostles and calls people into public representative ministry to acknowledge the complexity of association and of the construction of the spiritual environment, and yet to be confident in proclaiming a faith that owns difference and unity through a dynamic of fraction and wholeness focussed in the Word and Sacrament of Jesus the Christ.

The second theological element is the key role of vision – signs and words which point to ever greater possibilities and articulate confidence in the power of the forgiveness of falling short and the resurrection of brokenness to become the material of eternity. This provides a comforting and encouraging perspective to every endeavour of private faith, association and partial construction of public space. Thus there needs to be a dynamic between vision (with its special words and signs) and practical organisation of particular "spaces."

The danger of democracy is that it invites people to "buy in" to vision for limited periods, and restricts vision to the questions people ask. Scripture and the Gospel of the kingdom provide much more taxing and exhilarating challenges, rooted in the inner life of prayerful reflection, rather than in externals. The latter reduces judgement to matters of taste and fashion – a reactive survival technique rather than a deeper desire for a glory sensed but not fully seen. This is something that can only be constructed by faith in the gift of goodness from beyond our limited struggles – the transforming gift of new life. In this sense truth is not about patterns that make sense of what can be seen and experienced: rather truth is a richer mystery that is glimpsed but never fully grasped. It is in this way that association needs to be recognised as an art rather than as a science.

Two contrasting classical traditions help to put the role of public representative ministry and the tools of hierarchy and vision in perspective.

For ancient civilisation the questions of truth and the pressures of pluralism in terms of human experiences and ideas led to two approaches. Plato came to believe that most creatures would only have the time, or ability, or inclination, to handle parts of the truth – those portions most relevant to themselves and their particular situation[1]. Yet truth was all embracing, and was needed to provide connection, coherence and stability. The solution came in the form of Plato's notion of the Philosopher King, who could see the larger picture and greater possibilities, and help mediate the purer light to those who inevitably lived in the shadows of their own limitations. This model of operation privileges wisdom. The task of the wise is to guide those whose partial views can only be described as opinions. This is not easily achieved through democracy, since an agglomeration of opinions can proclaim itself to be the truth. Thus Plato favoured a stronger model of authority to shape and steer – though this too becomes a command economy, since the Wise Philosopher is trained to see more clearly in terms of evaluation of the present and assessment of possibilities in the future. In this approach, truth is primary and mere opinion is dangerous. Thus the role of law is crucial in embodying the wisdom of truth, which requires conformity.

By contrast Aristotle sought to recognise that each part of creation was pregnant with a potential that could develop to fulfil the greater purposes of the whole. Every portion was a key participant with its own unique potential contribution. Truth emerged from the discernment of every vocation and its connecting creatively and appropriately with other portions, towards the full fruition of the whole. On this model, representative oversight was not focussed in the articulation and application of the truth, but rather acts as a servant encouraging and modelling a process of discernment and appropriate engagement. Representative oversight encourages vocational development as a part of the unfolding of the truth.

For the Christian church these two models represent two poles which have had particularly influential effects among a much wider range of possibilities discernible in ecclesiastical history. In fact the authority of truth given by Jesus the Christ as Son of God needs to be acknowledged as determinative and overarching. But the truth embedded in every person given the gift of life (John 1$^{1\text{-}14}$), is a flicker of light that requires careful nourishment, interpretation and embracing in the fuller glory of eternity - as witnessed by Jesus the Son of Man. The art of leadership in the church will be to provide the focus of a person who embodies the truth and offers it through word and sacrament, while offering also a process of vocational discernment and guidance for private faith, associational life and intimations of an all encompassing glory.

In the Acts of the Apostles there are models of the workings of this double pattern of association in the interplay between small groups meeting in private homes, and the public proclamation by authorised leaders in the Temple courts (Acts 2$^{46\text{-}47}$, 5$^{12\text{-}14}$ and 5^{47} - 6^{1}). A significant point of connection was the common practice of breaking bread, the associational activity where Jesus brought together fellowship with Himself, with the Father, and with the sacrifice of the lamb that embraces God's people in the new life of salvation.

This bringing together of authority and invitation, leadership and participation, external discipline and internal exploration, comes not through the despotism advocated by Plato, nor through the more organic unfolding of the force of creation unveiled by Aristotle, but rather through conversation and the enacting of fellowship (the ministry of word and sacrament). This ministry needs to operate particularly in the public arena[2], with a desire to discern how associations can interact and greater agendas be fulfilled. This allows engagement with what has been given (the Son of God), discernment of opinions, and exploration of how these partial views can better relate to more ultimate possibilities (relationship with the Son of Man). Love and grace together enable new life.

The task of the church is to offer arenas for this kind of public engagement – to refine opinion and private faith, to encourage associations and cross fertilization between them, and to enable connection between the ultimate Truth of Jesus the Christ and the risky, exploring mission of Jesus the Son of Man.

CHAPTER 5

The Bankruptcy of Democracy

Enormous hope is invested in the project of liberal democracy. This is best exemplified by F Fukuyama's book "The End of History" which argued for the enduring and all embracing triumph of the liberal democratic project as the bedrock of a new and richer global civilisation[1]. A more practical example would be the mantra of the American Government under President George Bush that foreign policy and military power should combine to speed the path towards liberal democracy. For countries such as Iraq or Afghanistan such a project is based upon the presupposition that political organisation and human values depend upon a universal acknowledgement of human rights and mechanisms of participation and consultation. This ideal scenario is provided through the system of each adult person having a vote.

There are many problems with this almost uncritical faith in liberal democracy. Besides the historical and philosophical criticisms of such an extreme thesis as that proposed by Fukuyama[2], there is enormous evidence that the continuing proclamation of liberty, equality and fraternity is not delivering any of these qualities. Liberty is so circumscribed by the power of capital that "freedom" is continually exploited in a way that increases the gap between rich and poor, within nations and between nations[3].

Similarly, basic campaigns for gender equality and more participative working and political practices have had little impact upon the gross inequalities between men and women, in terms of expectations and earnings, or upon the conditions of many in paid employment, subject to continuing stress and uncertainties. The result is a disintegration of social networks, a collapse of community and a retreat from even an aspiration for fellowship into seemingly safer, more comfortable public spaces[4]. An opinion poll in 2007 showed that in the United Kingdom only 16% of people trusted politicians. Clergy scored 29%[5]. There is an alarming disconnection between people and politics, as there is between people and institutional forms of organisation. For example, in the United Kingdom membership of churches, political parties and trades unions has plummeted. This is ironic at a time when the media revolution is providing the capacity for connecting people more easily and more comprehensively. In fact this kind of communications technology is chiefly appropriated for commercial or personal uses.

The roots of democracy spring from ancient Greece. The notion of rule by the people depended upon three key factors[6]. First, the small scale of the city state, so that discussion and decision making involved people in personal relationships – which enabled dialogue to continue for those whose views and values were overruled. Second, there was a clear distinction between economic organisation, through the oikos (household), which was a private matter, and political activity, through the polis (city), which provided a forum for discussion of common affairs regarding political matters. Today democratically elected governments have become controllers of the economy, and abandoned great areas of political discourse about values, lifestyle and overall aims to the private realm of atomised individuals and small interest groups. Third, participation in the political process was restricted to heads of households – a representative system that took seriously the roles and responsibilities of different members of the community, and recognised that only some people were in a position to have an overview of issues and a proper stake in the outcome of proceedings.

This is a very different model from the modern understanding of liberal democracy, which lacks these key refinements, resulting in the paradox that everyone is invested with rights and responsibilities, while, in fact, power resides in small elites with very limited accountability[7]. Thus politics has shifted from the activity of parties with strong grass roots connections, a cabinet style of leadership, and an ideological vision for future behaviours and values, to sofa government by a predominant, presiding personality, wielding enormous power and very loosely connected to party, parliament or grass roots. Much power in liberal democratic systems is exercised by commercial and cultural groups who exploit the possibility for wealth to shape "freedoms" for a variety of very narrow interests – keeping the great mass of people distracted by the relentless call to "fashions" and a continuing stress upon personal identity and survival. Thus the potential identified by philosophers such as Jurgen Habermas, for people to meet, debate and comment upon political issues has never been fully realised[8]. This free space was originally available in coffee shops and other arenas for people to meet outside of their normal interest groups, but as the system of government responded by giving the vote to more and more adult members of the population, so other mechanisms were developed to minimise the effectiveness of any serious steer coming from such conversations. In fact the mass society created by technology has become a manipulated society, under the sway of a sensationalist, localised media and the spin skills of sofa-Messiah political leaders.

The state promotes undifferentiated individualism in the public space, driven by the great emotive leveller of human rights but in fact creating a myriad of disconnected private spheres, from which people lack the skills, the vision or the means to engage with anything more macro. The occasional burst of web based activity around single issues illustrates the potential for technology to address this problem, and the paradoxical fact that individuals can only find energy and channels for greater connection around isolated, one-off matters.

The increasing sense of separation is a major force inducing stress: the collapse of enduring committed relationships, through family, work place or ideological commitment has the effect of filling the "freedom, equality and fellowship" of each person with the agenda of survival and a search for identity. This provides an atmosphere ripe for short cut solutions such as totalitarianism and fundamentalism – the ultimate appeal of a sofa-Messiah offered through the electronic media. Both Hitler and Mussolini came to power as the result of popular election.

Government becomes increasingly focussed upon issues of regulation and control – to provide a holding context for so many separated concerns and lifestyles. Cynicism arises among the electorate because the liberalism offered to individuals comes from a governmental system based upon one-way communication with voters, a very occasional opportunity to contribute, often around only two or three major issues at an election, and the frustration of political rhetoric being constantly contradicted by the needs of cohesion, social discipline and common life – unifying themes such as "multiculturalism" or "Britishness" are occasionally proclaimed as an attempt to bridge this gap, but they simply serve to identify the basic problems of incompatibilities more clearly.

With power moving so inexorably into the hands of unaccountable elites and experts, citizens have become consumers, reduced to the right to vote, very occasionally, on someone else's ideas. People are encouraged to be liberated worshippers of the god of Toleration, while being treated as fodder for other purposes. Liberal democracy has long ceased to be utopian – rather it is desperately pragmatic, balancing a discourse of selfish concern for rights and personal advantage (the low tax mantra) with a hollow agenda about community, cohesion and mutuality.

There is an enormous temptation for the Christian church to mirror this type of behaviour. The development of synodical government shadows the growth of the franchise in state political organisation, and there is an enormous pressure for church leaders to find a platform within the celebrity culture of sofa Messiahship offering "a way forward" for every value and viewpoint. Similarly the growth of bureaucracy and its sinews of regulations are providing a macro framework that is in danger of leaving localness and ordinary members feeling cynical and separated. The two great commandments are to love God (the biggest picture) and to love one's neighbour as oneself (i.e. the stranger and the needy). Both of these elements are being airbrushed out of the practice and the proclamation of churches, as the temptation is to concentrate upon the pressures which produce stress (money, stability, comfort, viability, secure identity) and thus behave like atomised, disconnected units seeking to survive in a world where these larger issues are handled by rhetoric or agencies "somewhere else."

In fact the Christian approach is based upon a very counter cultural model, ironically much closer to the characteristics of ancient Greek democracy. The teaching of Jesus is founded upon the image of a king and a kingdom. St Paul used the picture of a Head and a Body. Both depend upon authorised leadership or direction, the acknowledgement of difference, the dependence of every part of the whole, and the task of the overall enterprise to provide boundaries and focus for the various elements. Participation is not for the benefit of the particular individual, but for the benefit of the whole under the direction of those called and commissioned to represent the overall project. To encourage an individual to seek their own separated identity, or to use their resource for their own benefit (e.g. lower taxation) would be totally incompatible with this model.

Resources for this counter cultural Christian approach are found in what God has given: scripture, creeds, sacraments and an authoritative ministry of oversight which guarantees these non negotiable, foundational and formational ingredients. The resources provided by the analysis of human experience and aspiration need to be processed through this purifying and formational sieve. The tendency is to operate in the reverse way – mirroring a world of phone-ins, opinion canvassing and liberated individualism, and reinterpreting these primal resources in that light. The doctrine of the fall is a reminder that human eyes see as through a glass darkly. Sin and selfishness pollute the instinct for love and connectivity. Only grace freely given from outside of our natural context can forgive and fulfil.

Much of this tension is addressed in the public liturgy of the church where participants bring all kinds of fragments and need to access the cohesion of the Gospel in a way which allows a particularised, limited but good – enough appropriation. In this sense the liturgy must always remain unfinished – in its contents and in its enactment – while at the same time offering connection with coherence and completion. The Christian life remains a dynamic between law and grace, struggle and salvation. The connector is loyalty to a head, a king, a person, and to a process of engagement which is always inviting exploration and ownership of incompletion desiring fulfilment.

Augustine recognised that this process and the Good News in this Person, depended upon ownership of sin – the lust for selfish security and satisfaction; the pressure of mortality and the instinct for life which resists it: and the miracle of "natality" – the human capacity to create new hope, new ideas, new life, even in the midst of adversity and death[9]. This latter ability to bring to birth new life often flows from the forgiveness which can open up opportunities beyond moments of failure, and from a deep faith in greater possibilities (for the whole of life – an instinct bastardised by capitalisms attempt to redirect it according to the forces of fashion.)

By contrast, the stance of sofa Messiahship has collapsed into a string of promises to "complete" – assuring that "mistakes" or "accidents" will never happen again; proposing "solutions" to economic and social issues that in fact will be perennial; rarely admitting to failure or the reality of incompleteness. The emphasis upon good management creates a dependency upon efficient bureaucracy and an atomisation of those managed – who are offered the compensation of private space for their own faith and agenda.

Religious fundamentalism operates in an identical way. There is an abandonment of honesty about the enduring nature of sin, the reality of mortality and the instinct for grace within imperfection rather than by abolishing it. The "superlative" culture of a rhetoric which could not cope with the merely "good enough" and the mysterious dynamic of the wheat and the tares (Matthew 13$^{24\text{-}30}$), the mixed economy of God's salvation. Many religious revivals begin with the challenge "Repent" but then provide such a controlled system of response that they can only function through continual dissolution and regroupings.

There is an Anglican tradition of provisonality, not-knowing and seeking the truth in dialogue which is important for both church and political society in the present climate[10]. Structures of parish, deanery, diocese, province and Anglican Communion provide contexts for engagement with a Person and a process that acknowledges hierarchical authority in terms of the basic ingredients and the controlling narrative, but invite local, personal and group reflection, engagement and exploration. Like the person of the Messiah, the process is open, calling to freedom through sacrifice rather than self- fulfilment, offering equality which is mystical rather than measurable and fellowship which is always subject to fraction and input from new participants. Bureaucracy, benchmarking and efficient organisation of resources and opportunities will always be secondary.

Contemporary liberal democracy is increasingly exposed as bankrupt. It presents oversimplified and over ambitious conceptions of social coherence and political identity, and works by the manipulation of separated, stressed individuals. The temptation to deal in solutions is rarely resisted, and the resulting failure to deliver is the germ of growing cynicism and dissatisfaction. The Pauline system was much closer to the roots of the democratic aspiration: small units, authoritative representative leadership, and a clear differentiation between private economic responsibilities and the need of the community for coherence through common views and values (Acts 4). The workings of this system gave space for conflict, synodical discussion and continuous dialogue (Acts 15). Human living was clearly unfinished, without the miraculous gift of grace in the person of the Messiah – who modelled personal engagement not just through His own image, action and discourse, but also through those processes and persons He empowered to represent His kingdom project. A spirit of wholeness emerged in human hearts to enable the forgiveness, fraction and flourishing that guided pilgrims through this earthly vale towards each other and towards their final destination.

This Christian model is wary of a simple, single controlled public space – inhabited nervously by individuals expected to find more personal identity within their own private sphere. Rather the church calls for a series of interconnected, differentiated public spaces, where different kinds of public faith can be contested and focussed. The bankruptcy of a call for a monolithic liberal democracy needs the medicine of a plurality of islands of encounter (often around feasting and festivals), communing through faith in a common Person and process.

In terms of a Christian witness about the nature of public space, there needs to be a number of responses. First, to provide a model in the way our own public space is organised. Second, to promote models in existing areas of public space which illustrate our core principles and practices. Third, to engage with networks and agencies trying to operate within public space as presently constituted. Fourth, to exemplify the richness of association through families, cells, local and regional activities.

CHAPTER 6

Leadership and Followership

When faith is pushed into the realm of the private, and public space is presented as a "neutral" arena within which all faiths coexist but no dominant ideology is owned the art of leadership and the role of followership easily model the prevailing pattern.

Celebrity culture and sofa Messiahship become ways of conducting a one-way relationship that solicits support, operates through the forces of fashion, and promises success by impersonal identification combined with a boost in confidence for the crafting of a private identify and lifestyle. In terms of church leadership a parallel pattern is emerging. However, because the scale and resourcing relating to church leadership tends to be so much smaller, the practical outcome is that leadership depends upon the much more direct approval of the led. Leadership works by developing a contract with followers, and in smaller scale operations this will be always subject to revision and reformulation according to the needs and aspirations of those being offered oversight.

In this sense leadership has become dependent upon the personal skills of interpreting experience and offering acceptable paths of response. Whereas traditional leadership was exercised through established values, symbol systems, dogmas, and disciplines – meaning that the leader was clearly a representative of something much greater, the personalisation of encounter though the mass media means that leadership is exercised through the quality of performance: making the personality more significant than that which they claim to represent[1].

This accords with the contemporary trust in shifting scenes and process, rather than in more enduring marks and restrictive disciplines.

There has been a major shift from tradition and a notion of "givens", to experience and the power of exploration and new creations. The first was epitomised by Dionysius and the notion of a celestial hierarchy – with degrees of value, and the second by Copernicus and a cosmology of universal laws embracing everything equally[2]. Calvin represents an interesting moment of this shift. Once the objective effectiveness of the sacraments was questioned, then the tools and the role of the minister depended not on faithful administration of what had been given, but rather upon the ability to interpret, codify and provide a frame for testing and shaping experience. The emphasis was upon "your faith will save you": the bewildering variety of experiences thus engendered required much more sophisticated mechanisms of evaluation and control[3].

The mantle of Calvin still hangs over the contemporary world of liberal capitalism, as both governments and churches offer leadership that is based upon interpretation, codification and control. On the scale of national government, as argued above, this issues in a massive exercise of pseudo consultation and steady manipulation to satisfy the demands of powerful lobby forces.

Within the life of the church the issue is less straightforward. Smaller public spaces, such as congregations, provide a place where negotiation is more necessary. And as resources from beyond the congregation have diminished, at least in Anglican terms, thereby undermining any semblance of independence for the minister, there is increasing pressure for leadership to be exercised according to the demands of the led. The classical resources of scripture, sacraments and creeds are reshaped according to local taste. Increasingly the key factor in giving a parish identity is the personality of the local priest and the outcome of negotiations between that particular leader and those being led. The key relationship is no longer between the representative of the church as a universal corporation and the local. Rather, the key relationship is between the personality of the leader and the people in that particular community. This model is transferred to other levels of ecclesial operation, so that the needs and perceptions of particular contexts provides the shaping and agenda for the exercise of leadership, and for the use of the traditional resources given to the church by Her Lord.

This means that people only gather round, and invest authority in, those images, practices and styles of leadership that meet the needs of their personal faith journey. Private faith tends to become magnified by finding a small, but more public, space within which it can be celebrated and enhanced, but rarely broken and re-made. When the expression and explanation of faith in a public sense was dictated more narrowly by geography, then both of these elements needed to be present. Modern mobility and liberalism provides privileged space simply for the positive element – often fairly uncritically. People choose to travel to find spaces of comfort, and to avoid challenge.

The result is that leadership in the church is not rooted in representing the church catholic as the primary site of reality; nor is it rooted in interpreting the word as the privileged place of revelation; nor is it rooted in the Sacraments as objective encounters with the purifying, re-making power of God; rather it depends upon establishing a contract of commitment to a person and the way in which they give messages and provide images. This shift endorses the growth of individualism and localism encouraged by the forces of globalisation as a way of keeping individuals isolated and disconnected. Similarly it coheres with a reaction against privileging a single text, and invites input from a variety of texts, including those of differing human lives. It mirrors the effect of democracy in engineering a transfer of power from the king to the body of the people (though failing to find adequate systems to maintain the kind of organic connection which monarchy enables). The oneness of God is perforated by the plurality of human experience, and the minister has moved from using specified tools to measure and evaluate the latter, to concentration upon managing without radical judging. Understandably the minister as a person holds back from exercising the critique and judgement that more objective resources might provide. The task of leadership concentrates upon managing resources (including human resources) and image for that particular group. The values and views of wider society provide a backdrop inviting comment, and often criticism, but there are few mechanisms for serious discussion of differences – either within the congregation or in terms of dialogue with other agencies in the community. Much of this kind of behaviour is reinforced by the parish share system, which encourages gathering together for the survival of the group, and by the behaviour of dioceses as greater agents of management, with "vision and values" reduced to soundbite straplines and little evidence of serious study to discern deeper perspectives regarding the life of society at large.

In this model Kingship, or Headship of the Body, becomes localised and privatised. The "public" expression of the Gospel reflects a culture within which faith is essentially a private matter for consenting adults (and sometimes their children) designed to have no significant effects beyond those of that particular group. Authority is increasingly in the hands of the majority voice within each local grouping, so that, as with other expressions of liberal democracy, difference and deviance is to be dismissed into other, unconnected, private realms. The responsibility members of a body or a kingdom feel for all the other parts, whatever their difference or apparent deviancy, is conveniently abandoned. Instead of the pain of serious dialogue, wrestling with the potentially lifegiving mysteries of fraction and forgiveness, there is an appeal for alliance with like minded groups – thereby reinforcing the "private", closed expression of faith, and withdrawing from the risky and robust public space completely. At the Areopagus Paul made sure he told the story of the Resurrection, even if it meant leaving loose ends and randomly scattered seeds, together with the experience of rejection.

By contrast church is becoming a bottom-up activity: a confessional association of believing individuals giving voluntary allegiance to an effective local leadership. The new sacrament of seriousness is the giving of money, rather than a common ritual and dogma embracing cooperating communities committed to offering a model of fulfilling belief and behaviour to a struggling world, under the authority of a hierarchy of ministers significant only because of their commission to represent the One. The church exists most fully not in its Head/King, and His representative persona and practices, but rather in authorisation given by consenting members to local leadership and an operation measured by the blessings it brings to its adherents[4].

In the early nineteenth century there were great debates about the condition of England – particularly the collapse of community with the growth of the industrial revolution, and a fear that the ordering of traditional society was disintegrating[5]. A number of people initiated symbolic schemes to address this situation. Robert Owen established model villages and workplaces. Coleridge advocated the importance of the clergy, to help to mature civilisation in terms of values and vision, through cultural leadership. Thomas Arnold was an advocate of education to provide a common sense of belonging and believing. Carlyle endorsed the importance of heroes as leaders through example and inspiration. Their aims were not to develop organisational harmony, and each tended to be wary of the claims of liberal democracy as it was beginning to emerge. Rather, their concerns were with the spiritual nourishment of citizens, to better enable personal development within the context of the associations, and within the society, that provided formation and the opportunities for fulfilment. The whole was more important than the parts, and ways needed to be explored, particularly in the areas of work, culture, education and history, that could help individuals discover their proper identity and role in relation to others, and in relation to wider society.

Their key methods provide a salutary challenge to twenty-first century concentration upon the analysis of human experience and the management of liberty through bureaucracy and technology. Each made a foundational appeal to the study of the past. Much in human nature is enduring: progress is often illusory. Models of organisation and aspiration in history are rich in resources. This presents a powerful challenge to a society which is so future orientated that the study of history is sometimes undermined by a political correctness that despises hierarchy, tradition and sacrificial service as undermining of the myth of equality.

Second, each of these nineteenth century pioneers gave priority to engagement with the poor. There was a strong gospel imperative about compassion and effective charity that had enormous influence across Victorian society. This engagement was predicated upon the supposition that sacrifice of self and generous service of others was a path of fulfilment in spiritual terms, and the preferred way of pilgrimage towards the heavenly kingdom. By contrast, in the contemporary Church, such prodigious commitment to sacrifice and service of others is something more likely to be expressed by rhetoric rather than carefully chosen actions. The sacrificial service of society by characters such as Shaftsbury and Wilberforce provoked a response in both giver and receiver, and nurtured a spirituality of mutuality and commonness in the great scheme of things. These visions appealed to a quality of relationship, although often they reverted to dependence upon institutional rigidity.

Third, leadership was unashamedly hierarchical and directive. Confident in common standards and markers that were hardly negotiable, and which provided a determining context for all: leaders and led. Engagement and habit provided the bedrock: schemes and analysis were always secondary elements. The notion of a common life for all embracing a variety of roles, authorities and responsibilities provided a public space for private faith to be both nurtured, and formed further through owning deeper connection and common purpose with others.

Every retreat into narrow privacy would be seen as depriving the world of that potential contribution and new life[6]. Means and models needed to be developed to invite these contributions particularly by providing public space which could embrace a variety of views and offerings. This kind of leadership appeals to the depths of the inner life, rather than simply to the management of material existence. In this way there can be an authority about a call to sacrifice and service which is authenticated in the act of offering. This would be the experience of liturgy and of love expressed through the sacrament of marriage.

The response of the follower is to an agenda which resonates with the Gospel of eternity – its scriptures, sacraments and creeds. The leader is merely a representative of this cleansing and lifegiving agency – and authority is exercised through these forms, of which the minister's performance is just one element.

There is common ground for leader and led – a mutuality that embraces differences of role as well as differences of gift and circumstance. The Oneness of God and the all embracingness of His Kingdom provides the key. Without this key, more human resources draw us into the creation of private faith in narrow, privileged, separated spaces. God's oneness with all of creation will constantly break down the more limited togetherness we inevitably create. In this sense leadership will need to be prophetic and challenging, as well as pastoral and comforting. Public space provides the arena for both to flourish as instanced by a cross on a key highway outside the city wall.

CHAPTER 7

Inner Life and Its Outward Expression

Christianity provides a series of challenging perspectives on the understanding of public spaces, and the role of faith within it.

Greek mythology saw the gods as immortal. Human beings were mortal, the mere playthings of the gods. The Christian Gospel reversed this perception, and claimed that human beings were called to immortality, while the world was transient and mortal. Thus public space is a secondary, temporary area, part of the pilgrimage of the human soul. The presupposition of this theology is that of a deep, hidden inner life of the soul, which passes as a pilgrim through the fleshliness of mortal being, but which is formed for eternity. Thus the discourse and activity of the public realm provided markers and signs relating to a more hidden transaction – that of the work of the spirit.

Similarly, the Roman emphasis upon the past, particularly the Founders, provided a determinative steer for activity in the public space. Christianity was focussed upon a Founder, but only as foundation for the construction of a new heaven and a new earth. The realm of public space was preparatory, not determinative. The key working was that of the spirit calling out repentance, receipt of new life, and confidence in the world to come.

The penultimacy of the public realm, and the priority given to the inner life points to what Paul described as the groaning of the whole creation in its seeking of perfection (Romans 8). He develops this theology by distinguishing between the flesh and the spirit or body. The inner life is not simply some form of therapy so as to better adjust to the apparently measurable marks of effective material life. Rather, the inner life is a place of confession of limitations, receipt of new life and a transformation in terms of self-understanding and ultimate direction. The faith thus engendered is focussed upon One God and Father of us all (Ephesians 4). It must be given witness in the public realm.

The necessary activities of measuring, planning and targeting performance is underlain by more mysterious energies and aims only partly realisable in this world, yet crucial as signs of direction and encouragement. Thus, this hidden dimension of human beings cannot be simply consigned to the area of 'private' faith: rather this elemental energy of every human soul requires an outlet for examination, contribution and correction. This will happen through public liturgy, and through political endeavour to shape public life accordingly.

The method does not involve a crude parading of achievements in order to invite political or commercial support. Rather there needs to be a humility which recognises the provisionality and flexible nature of any achievements, and the need for ongoing reflection, reshaping and receiving of new life. Glory is given by, and to, God: it is not a human construct. This differential encapsulates the distinctiveness of the Christian approach to the construction of the second environment that we term public space. It is essentially a spiritual construct, with secondary and provisional material expressions. The key organ is prayful reflection, rooted in scripture, sacraments and creeds, and employing these 'given' resources as tools to interpret and reshape human experience and aspiration.

An urgent task for secular government is to recapture the centrality of humble reflection and probing prayer. Sadly, the witness of churches has often colluded with the privatisation of these essential resources – to the effect of offering prayers 'for society and those in political authority' without serious ownership of the responsibility that such an inner life demands in terms of attempting to enflesh the values and insights petitioned. He took flesh and engaged with the rule of Pontius Pilate.

The Gospel brings some distinctive insights into public life. First is the doctrine of sin and the Fall. There is a basic flaw in human beings, which needs to be owned and then healed by the gracious love of God in Jesus Christ. This is the bedrock of an inner life ever seeking to be honest about failings and limitation, and owning the provisionality of our constructions in this world. This contrasts markedly with the amazing optimism of Huxley, the populariser of Darwin's theory of evolution, with his contention that when man fell, he fell upwards, i.e., there is a basic presupposition of progress and improvement whatever the setbacks. This optimism, underwritten by Hegelian dialectic, is a powerful driver in the construction of public space in the twenty first century. It conveniently ignores the recent story of Fascism, Communism, world wars and unprecedented poverty and disease across the planet. Faith in human ability to progress drives the Green Movement, and the danger of a return to the perspective that the planet represents immortality (if properly preserved by human ingenuity) while human lives are transitory and small parts in this larger enterprise.

Christian preaching begins in Jesus and in John the Baptist with the word 'Repent'. There is much that needs challenging and changing. Moreover, suffering and death remain defining experiences, which can bring purification rather than simple extermination if embraced with an inner trust in God's mercy and grace. God's economy is not one of unending progress in terms of material existence and its public expression. Rather God's economy operates through the heart and the inner recesses of reflection, wonder and hope. This inner life demands expression through the penultimacy of human being on earth as a step towards fulfilment beyond.

The doctrine of sin and the fall is complemented by the doctrine of forgiveness, perhaps the most distinctive part of the Gospel of Jesus the Christ. Forgiveness can open up the barriers created by sin and limitation by accepting what has been and yet inviting new possibilities to emerge – not in spite of, but through that which disappoints and destroys. This positive engagement with sin and failure, trusting in transformation as a gift to enable new possibilities, is very different from the world of careful calculation and construction using only tried and tested materials. Compassion takes precedence over the desperate attempts to create fairness and equality which are the hallmarks of public policy so often. Forgiveness involves letting go of control, and trusting the inner forces of love to heal and create new opportunities. The challenge to the Church is how to give precedence to this spiritual exploration in her own life, and as a model for a more general construction of public space. A clue to an appropriate response lies in the recognition that before a more recent emphasis upon public space as an arena for economics – the ordering of the exchange of gifts and services, to underwrite private lifestyles – there has been a long tradition of seeing such space as the place for culture (including politics in the classical sense of the debate about values and overall direction). These activities have been increasingly privatised, although the continuation of some public funding for the arts is witness to a residual recognition of the value of both the inner life and of its public expression.

Christianity has provided an important impetus to liberal democracy in its insistence upon the precious uniqueness of every person, but it roots this insight in a call to conversation, prayerful reflection, concern for the construction of public space and a sacrificial offering of self to be an agent of the Kingdom in this transitory life. Thus the inner life is the bedrock of private faith, associations for formation, community connections and the aspiration for eternity. Personal faith is formed by, and contributes towards, the corporate life of human kind at many levels. Too often questions about such things as the meaning of life, suffering, the power of love, the desire for healing,…are no longer part of the official discourse of public life in liberal democracies. People can pick and chose possible approaches from a free market of religions and ideologies. The inner life is a personal resource.

Yet the funding of culture in the public space is a sign of hope. Truth, beauty, imagination, reflection, awe…are all elements of inner being that can be shared through public performance, exhibition and conversation. These deeper discourses are both the energy of the human heart, and the stuff of Christian liturgy. There is an urgent need for such an agenda to be more self consciously present within the mix of factors which are encouraged to participate in the construction of public space. Thus the second environment human beings are uniquely equipped to create can be expressed not simply through private faith and practice (values and lifestyle) within a common holding environment of organising the exchange of goods and services (an economy treated as a political framework). Rather, the inner life of each soul can be invited to grow through the relationships of association, a desire for ever greater connectivity and a spiritual impetus that infuses every element of public life. Hegel approached a similar vision with his notion of world – spirit[2], but in the sense of the Christian Gospel this is much more localised, incarnated, as an expression of something material and expressed through catholic order.

The contribution of the Christian Church is to enable small communities of formation based around the interplay of disciplined reflection in the inner life (prayer through Jesus Christ) and outward expressions of the leading of the common spirit in terms of practice and corporate life. A further network of such communities provides an opportunity for the construction of a catholic (all embracing) ordering of human life, based upon similar disciplines of prayful reflection. Each enterprise gives priority to formation through scripture, sacrament, creed and the oversight of an authorised ministry.

Besides offering light and leaven in the public arena more broadly, these enterprises will both provide models of how cultural activities and thoughtful inner reflection might inform more overtly political and economic organisation, and also equip practising Christians to be agents of these processes through their own witness and performance beyond the life of the Church itself. Such a cocktail provides space for giving and receiving, being affirmed and also challenged, having selfishness rubbed off and sacrifice grown in its place. These dynamics need to be at the heart of the construction of public space as well as central to the formation of Christians and their communities. There needs to be room for an inner life within public institutions and practices.

The big pictures (love God – the whole project: love neighbour – the needy and the stranger) need focussing by much deeper means than the movement and organisation of material resources. There need to be places to nourish the disciplines of the inner life, people skilled to offer oversight and encouragement, and prophetic practice of both spiritual discernment and its tangible expression. Inner life needs freedom and focus. It also needs space to be still, and sometimes stalled, in the wilderness of not knowing and not seeing. This is the hardest, darkest place to plumb, but the one that yields the deepest and most encouraging insights. The way of the cross is more than Christian rhetoric: it witnesses to the journey of Jesus that shows the triumph of light over darkness and of life over death. This coheres with the deepest instincts in human beings, but instincts so deep that they can easily remain hidden and unexamined. It is through engagement with the most testing and dispiriting of issues and contexts that real hope and direction are nourished. This requires the discipline of waiting and watching – not simply rushing out a plan to put things right. Such reflective, humble, struggling space is crucial to a healthy public domain and yet it is something almost always denied, swept away by the power of technology to communicate and to organise change. Sometimes public space needs to be constructed around the pain of pausing, not knowing, and seeking a deeper perspective[1]. The Garden of Gethsemane is central to the Christian Gospel but easily glossed over. The ability to live with brokenness, despair and struggle as part of the resources for constructing public space requires a culture of public faith that recognises the centrality of prayer, the realism of the dynamic between death and resurrection, and the role of priestly ministry alongside that of political organisation. Symbols, music, art – provide tools for such priestly ministry in the public domain – the Gospel gives coherence and the confidence of blessing. The struggle for meaning involves hearts as well as heads, and requires inner reflection alongside effective organisation.

CHAPTER 8

Christians and the Construction of Public Space

In the Book of Genesis creation begins as a formless chaos, and the creator constructs ordered space by separating out light and dark, day and night, male and female – a host of contrasting, different elements. Every element is given life by the ruach or spirit of God, and thus there is an underlying oneness and connection between things that are apparently different and separate. To discern the underlying oneness is a spiritual exercise, learning to perceive a common and connecting force beneath the physical, surface manifestations of difference.

The story of the fall, and the problem of knowledge and the choices of good and evil are focussed in trees and an apple. A sign that the presenting materialism of life easily assumes precedence. Thus the reaction of Adam and Eve to the gift of knowledge is to cover their bodies with fig leaves. The underlying spiritual forces are ignored, and human living concentrates upon survival in the physical environment.

The narrative is illustrative of the present context characterised by the privatisation of faith and the management of public space by the application of knowledge and moral choices to immediate issues of material existence. Spiritual discernment of underlying and more mystical perspectives is a personal matter and of no real relevance to the practical tasks at hand.

This issue was explored by Plato with his famous image of the cave. Human kind tends to look inwards, viewing shadows on the wall, because the true light is in fact behind us. Only those who have the courage to turn round and risk looking into the light will see things as they truly are, and can offer a richer interpretation of the shadowy existence of most of their peers. This image is the basis of a rich mystical tradition, and echoes something of the approach in the Gospel of John – the presupposition that behind the signs such as bread, wine, water, weddings, or the apprehension of an adulteress, are the deeper realities of life. The signs are shadows that require deeper reflection and interpretation. God calls out some apostles to take this risk of deeper engagement with the source of life and offer interpretation and guidance to others, particularly in the everydayness of existence. Apples, weddings and arguments are some of the biblical images redolent with meanings of a deeper grace and connecting discourse. Nature needs to be seen as part of a supernatural project: this life is made to be embraced into eternity. These insights are the ingredients of understanding and constructing a public space that expresses this truth and enables people to explore it further.

Similarly, Aristotle distinguishes between matter, the living material of creation, and form, the potential which each element of creation is called to fulfil in a manner that meets the purpose of the Divine creator. Once again, experience of the natural world can only be properly understood by the spiritual discernment of the underlying purposes and potential of every element imbued with the gift of life.

From the Reformation and the development of political philosophy in the sixteenth century, there has been an increasing confidence in discerning the meaning and purpose of life according to analysis of human experience and organisation, with a variety of views and schools regarding the status and function of any underlying master narrative in terms of spiritual purposes and an agenda evolving into eternity. The twenty first century operates through a liberal democratic idea of the 'normative' that places the pragmatism of designing and distributing the fig leaves of security and identity at the centre, and leaves listening to the voice of God as an optional extra for those who care to pay attention to that kind of thing.

This is not a simple choice. Nature does hold key signs about the purpose of creation. In Jesus Christ the incarnation exemplifies mortal human fleshliness becoming the stuff of eternity. The issues for Christians concern matters of priorities and practices.

To look inwards, the discipline of spiritual direction, is to discern a deeper oneness than our attempts to handle difference through organisations is able to recognise. This deeper perception can give a confidence about living with tension and even apparent incompatibility. In the nineteenth century an Anglican theologian, Julius Hare, made an important distinction between civilisation and cultivation[1]. Civilisation is the necessary work of constructing the world through political, economic and social organisation. To provide suitable forms for expressing the potential in each human life. This is the task of the state and of a whole host of secular, human-focussed associations. By contrast, cultivation is the art of opening minds to see more deeply into the signs of nature, of the times, of scripture, creed and sacrament. Cultivation requires skilled leadership. Coleridge called for a clerisy – people to help nourish a richer mindset to seek beauty, grace, peace and hopefulness, as a perspective within which the construction of civilisation should take place.

The art of cultivation is the task of opening eyes to the underlying spiritual current of creation for greater possibilities than the experiences of human living might deem possible, or even likely. It is an attempt to appeal to the hopes of the heart and the instinct for love: the spiritual capacity to transcend mere materialism and enter a reality with others and with the creator and sustainer of the world.

Too often the Church becomes drawn into an identity and a role defined by playing a soothing part in the constructing of civilisation – providing care and comfort to casualties and at points of stress: offering encouragement around matters of joy and hope. Jesus gave a great deal of attention to these areas in his own ministry. People often experience life as being like sheep without a shepherd (Mark 6[34]). However, Jesus was strident and piercing in the challenges he offered to those who shaped mindsets and established goals: Pharisees, governors, political and religious leaders. This is the tradition of prophecy: the underlying oneness of creation demands that these practices, ideologies and ways of being religious which operate through oppression, separation and destruction of 'others' and 'otherness' need to be challenged to seek more carefully an awareness of the deeper purposes and possibilities in God's intentions. The method employed revolves around the identification and interpretation of signs: of the times, and from the tradition[2]. The interplay between the two sets of resources often provides the spark of new light and richer possibilities.

The priest safeguards the purity of the signs given through scripture, sacrament and creed. The prophetic voice is vital to ensuring a robust interplay between the gifts God has provided, and the needs and problems of contemporary living. The pastor offers a witness to the ever present love of God which rises in human hearts to enable both survival, and sharper spiritual insight and the energy to act accordingly for change and transformation to occur.

As the state and voluntary associations of all sorts fulfil vocations to organise public space to enable action to be ordered most effectively, it is imperative that the deeper insights of spiritual discernment and discipline are offered to inform, critique and sometimes directly challenge the ever present tendency towards instrumental efficiency according to the canons of immediate human experience, at the expense of the much more difficult, costly and often uncertain act of seeking guidance and shaping for the whole enterprise, and every precious part within it, according to God's greater purposes.

Classically the Church has tackled this commission through a public liturgy, whereby the signs from tradition and from 'today' interact to seek guidance and direction for individuals and communities. As the place of public liturgy has become marginalised there is an urgent need to rediscover the strategy of the early Church. Here a small minority focussed on liturgy as the central and life giving focus of their own life and witness, but then gave priority to establishing formational groups where participants experienced the new life of deeper reflection and careful interpretation of the signs. This empowered Christians to take appropriate prophetic action of critique and challenge in a pagan, idolatrous civilisation – within which 'cultivation' was a local or personal concern. Refusal to bear arms, or to engage in certain trades, alongside an absolute insistence upon sexual purity, provided signs that spoke volumes to every section of society, as did the refusal to honour the emperor, i.e., worship the prevailing system of political control and its privatisation of the spiritual life. The early Christians did not simply formulate values and views for themselves in private meetings, and then simply conform to the pagan cultures in which they were set. Their faith in the one God and Father of all impelled them to give priority to a witness that gave clear indications about the construction of public space and the second environment that human beings are empowered to create. This space could only function fruitfully in terms of the purposes of creation if issues of meaning and behaviour were addressed, not in terms of efficiency and functionality, but in terms of the cultivation of mindsets that gave priority to ultimate vision, humility to own failure, courage to be changed, a desire to give special care to the poorest, and hopefulness for eternity.

Some of this witness and mission was conducted by Apologists who contributed to the public debate about ideas, values and vision. From Paul on the Areopagus, to early Church fathers, there was an impressive stream of challenging critique of pagan society and an eloquent explanation of Christian understanding and life. This remains an urgent task in any society, and one that is in danger of serious neglect today. Not least because of a diversion of much Christian energy into the organisation of the institution: the construction of an internal Christian civilisation, within the safe space allotted to it by avowedly secular governments. History has noted and remembered this noble line of Apologists – the great minds and exponents of the faith. They form an important role model.

However, the real effectiveness of the Christian Gospel in the times of the Early Church was through the bold and the distinctive lifestyles of ordinary church members. Hence the priority St Paul gives to helping issues of formation around matters such as food, dress, sexual behaviour and civic responsibilities. This approach continued through the witness not just of the martyrs, but also through innumerable unrecorded lives that were counter cultural. A simple but clear indication of the power of spiritual discernment and a glimpsing of God's greater purposes, and a clear obedience to the teaching and self-sacrificing example of Jesus the Christ. Early Christians, in an oppressive, minority context, walked the way of the cross empowered by the bedrock of liturgy rooted in scripture, sacrament and creed, inspired by authoritative interpretation from those commissioned to exercise oversight, and emboldened by the grace and beauty discerned in the deeper spiritual current of God's grace to which this lifestyle offered connection.

There was an essential element of nonconformity about early Christianity: expressed in everyday ways by ordinary people. Christians made themselves distinctive because the concerns and priorities of God's deepest purposes in creation called for many approaches to human living to be challenged and changed. The place to start was not simply the macro – the debates of the Apologists. More fundamentally, the place to begin was in the exemplification of how human being might be best expressed: love made manifest in models of generous community, self sacrificing service and solidarity with the needy, and sexual purity and discipline. Each of these elements was radically subversive of a pagan culture obsessed with expressing individual freedom according to the canons of the most immediate pleasures of human experience. This witness was the leaven and light that transformed whole societies, and enabled the superstructure of intellectual apologetic to be properly understood and appropriated[3].

The method of challenging others to raise their sights higher in terms of community, connection and eternity, is rooted in small but significant acts of witness to how these values might be honoured, and all that undermines them be changed. Saying 'yes' to goodness and grace involves saying 'no' to forces of selfishness and superficial pleasures. The age of Toleration, in the Roman context, as in twenty first century liberal democratic cultures, gives little encouragement to the discipline of saying 'no'. Everything should be 'yes', as long as people take responsibility for their own private choices, and governments take responsibility for constructing the most effective and neutral holding mechanisms. The Gospel begins with the word 'Repent'. 'No' is foundational to Christian formation and witness. Literally a counter-cultural apologetic and lifestyle.

Civilisation often works by making people 'civil' – courteous, tolerant and well behaved. Anglicanism has often been expressed through this culture of politeness. In fact the

Gospel demands edge and tension – a prophetic bite to challenge and change – and to pay a cost by being an example and a conduit.

Focus on a Person and a process is rooted in prayerfulness and emerges in distinctive practice. This progression offers a template for Christian witness, and a challenge to the temptation to remain safely gathered around the Person who initiates this spiritual life, but who actually requires us to be pilgrims along the whole path. Matthew 25 is a reminder that entrance into eternity depends upon a formation that issues in small but significant action that exemplifies the spirit of creation in practice (feeding the hungry, visiting the prisoner, etc). The background messiness of debate and difference, within the organisation and without in terms of the more macro construction of public space will be ever present – to inform and inspire the outputs that construct a public space that is infused with the new life and hope of love and peace: seeds of eternity in sacrificial self giving between human beings across various kinds of boundaries – all emerging from a spiritual discipline and discernment.

CHAPTER 9

The Organisation of Public Space

Besides the discipline of spiritual reflection to discern the underlying currents of the creation and thus best cooperate with the possibility of formation for eternity in the Kingdom of Heaven, and the allied external expression of words and signs through which this life-giving current is made manifest as an invitation to others there is a foundational role in terms of modelling community – koinonia. Human beings grow through relationship, and the fullest expression of humanity is through the corporateness of reality: often struggling and partial in this world of competing forces and complex choices, but possible to taste and enact as a sign of the fulfilment in eternity.

Historically in the west, Christianity has taken a leading role in the construction of public space through the creation of community. A public faith has informed personal formation and believing, and shaped the practice of association at every level – from family to the operation of government, welfare and commerce. The residue of this legacy can be observed in rituals such as prayers at the beginning of parliamentary sessions, or on civic occasions. Gradually there has evolved a thorough separation of Christian faith from the formal workings of public life. The church provides liturgical space not for the interrelation of a myriad of Christian associations (or associations at least owning a Christian superstructure) but rather for the nourishment of the personal faith of those who choose to attend, and who take their own responsibility for the way in which such faith informs their public roles and engagement.

As government takes responsibility for the organisation and construction of public space through benchmarks and bureaucracy, this attempt to provide a neutral framework worthy of the god of Toleration serves not to set people free, but to create increasing stress, conflict, disconnection and cynicism. Attempts to create boundaries seem to stimulate challenge and complaint.

The Gospel brings a number of resources to the formation of creative communities. First is the recognition that all human relationships will be a mixture of altruism and selfishness, love and defensiveness, hope and despair.

Communities can only be founded upon the twin pillars of faith in their potential and forgiveness for their failures. A society founded upon rational legalistic efficiency is unable to handle forgiveness in this way of creating new life through the miracle of sheer grace. The focus upon fairness, measurement and clear boundaries to define public space undermines this vital part of the equation, and the effect is the collapse of community altogether. People retreat into small, sometimes single, units of defence, and rarely experience forgiveness outside of the most intimate of contexts. As church life gains most of its media exposure in relation to internal conflict and corruption, there is an urgent need for Christian witness to learn how to practice forgiveness and the creation of new opportunities in its community life: both as model and invitation to an unforgiving, self-righteous, rationalistic world. To forgive is an act of faith, and sometimes folly. Like risking crucifixion. Yet forgiveness forms the well of the deepest currents of the spirituality of new life which ever rises to cleanse and transform the dualisms and conflicts which seem to be inherent on the surface of creation – whether through the observation of nature, composed of light and dark or male and female, or through the tendency of human behaviour to be selfish and destructive of others. Faith in the possibility of recovery and new beginnings depends upon forgiveness. In a community context this is one of the most challenging tasks – as is evident in much of the New Testament – both among the disciples of Jesus, and in the ministry of St Paul. Faith in forgiveness accepts that there will be a tragic dimension to human being, which needs to be at the centre of a spiritual engagement with reality, and a sign of the depths from which new life can emerge.

One of the key images representing life in liberal democratic cultures is that of the shopping mall. This illustrates the apex of civilisation. A temple-like physical construction providing the most ideal environment to display and exchange goods and services. Every participant is a consumer, looking to nourish their own personal needs and dreams. Sometimes in small groups or families, but often alone.

A major feature of this sophisticated creation of public space is the plethora of places to eat and drink. A natural need is fulfilled with huge choice (actually very circumscribed by the dictates of fashion – a basic capitalistic ploy: hence the prevalence of a Starbucks culture). Many participate but there is no interpersonal relationship, let alone community. Everyone is served on their own terms.

This could be on equally accurate description of church life in the west in the early twenty-first century. A vast range of options available, though in practice rather circumscribed by the dictates of fashion (i.e. the ubiquitous music group!). People participate on their own terms, have their favourite outlets, but rarely interrelate to establish a working community. The increasing popularity of coffee after the service is a sign of a great need for interpersonal relationship in an environment that is assumed to be safe.

However, at the heart of Christian worship are the sacraments of baptism and Eucharist – baptism cleanses the individual, initiates them into the ownership of a public corporate faith, and accepts them as a member of a working community. Eucharist gathers that community to share bread and wine – broken, fallible parts drawn together in the mixture of joy and tragedy which is human being, and made into a Holy Communion through the grace of God administered by identification with the story of Jesus Christ living, dying and rising again. The outcome of both of these sacramental actions is the construction of a public space marked by the characteristics of a radical equality, despite the surface differences of appearance, aptitude and aspiration. The foundation of the Christian church in the Acts of the Apostles (Acts 2) is a vivid illustration that Holy Communion is a charter for Holy Communists[1] and that baptism is the great sacrament of equality. These sacraments provide a more realistic and robust basis of any possible expression of liberty, equality and fraternity.

Community can best be constructed around a table and the sharing of food and drink. Human social practice consistently bears witness to this truth, but rarely expresses its political and organisational implications. Much church history witnesses to a similar failure in Christian practice too. Yet, the most effective witness to public faith and its implications for the construction of public space and the second environment of meaning and direction, could come from this radical, transformative, illustrative embodiment of the potential private belief can deliver.

The allied discipline of stepping back for spiritual reflection that brings together the given signs of scripture, sacrament and creed with the need to consider contemporary signs critically, is the foundation upon which the practice of holy communion is based.

This is not simply a "churchy" way of meeting. Rather it provides a definitive and transformative model of how private faith can be continually challenged and purified so that it can be channelled appropriately in the construction of the kind of public space which coheres with the deepest undercurrents in creation. The creative forces cohere around the miraculous energy released through the disciplines of reflection, forgiveness and sacrifice of self. Each of these elements can open up moments of revelation and new birthing. They form a context for the outworking of prophetic insight and values, and a mechanism for continuing review and reshaping.

Baptism and eucharist provide a shaping for community which has political and economic implications, and provide a model for the wholeness of the ends to which any particular association aims. There is a need to construct public space with disciplines, resources and insights that have practical import for the necessary tasks of social and political organisation, providing signs and reference points, and empowering individuals and groups to embody and illustrate the potential thus revealed. The notion of interpenetration best exemplifies the common current of spiritual energy and awareness that is thus made clearer and more available as a resource and guide.

One of the most challenging features of community constructed on this sacramental basis is the limited place of understanding and measurable efficiency. Much depends upon faith, gift, the miracle of new possibilities, and the courage to act with grace and generosity. The core ingredient is re-membering a story as a definitive sign – and owning the incompleteness and imperfection of participants apart from the faith and forgiveness associated with engaging with this Person and this process. From such engagement emerges continuing reflection, prayerfulness and practice.

The making and enfleshing of such sacramental communities operates on a number of key formational sites. It provides a model for the intimacy of small associations along the lines of the oikos (family, kin, immediate networks).

Similarly it offers resources for the making of community between associations – the arena of the polis, the negotiation of the political, the values and views element of public space. Thirdly it provides a template for the creation of cultural life – through signs, moments and memories that form and re-form mindsets, and enable a more creative inhabitation of the other, more formally organised, sites of public organisation.

For each site of construction, private faith is nourished and yet drawn into deeper engagement, with others, and with the One Other who represents the ultimacy for which human hearts long.

In this way these sites are not called to negotiate some kind of interdependence based upon transparent benchmarks and areas of responsibility or accountability. Rather these key sites are embraced by a radical interpenetration of a common spirit, call and destination. Baptism and Eucharist are primarily sites of tasting beauty and transformation amidst the challenging realities of limitation and tragedy.

The implications for the practice and presentation of public liturgy are enormous. At a time when churches increasingly seek to conform to the expected comforts of a private front room, there is a need to offer space that is more challenging, focussed on the signs of tradition (cross, lectern, altar) and the signs of the times – with space for connection, re-formation and waiting in the wildernesses of apparent absence and uncertainty. Church must offer public space that makes private faith the energy of this kind of public vocation. The deepest currents of hope and tragedy can be held in hearts drawn into a greater vision, and yet able to handle these polarities through a process of signs, reflection and risk-taking action. Imagination and intuition can be raised and yet earthed in reality – for the salvation or health of the world.

CHAPTER 10

Identity and Community

Personal identity is revealed through relationship, and maturity depends upon the ability to be part of the widest context: community and its future. The outcomes of relationships are always uneven – as are the workings of nature. This unevenness, which evolves around the poles of consensus and conflict, can be managed partly by rational negotiation and planning. But the sheer complexity of human being, and the vibrant pluralism of personality and contexts means that the work of discovering identity and achieving maturity will involve dealing with conflict in a way that provides no simple, tangible resolution. In the construction of public space the twin resources are law, which judges and seeks to provide both correction and restraint, and the grace of toleration which simply accepts difference, generally within some basic limits.

At the heart of the Christian sacramental community lie the twin disciplines of confession and fraction. Besides managing difference through law or toleration, both of which are always subject to the pressures of incompletion and imperfection, the Christian Gospel invites the more radical step of beginning by owning the realities of limitation and perverseness – and then allowing them to be transformed through the giving of self in an act of sacrifice. This offering of self is not to a smarter scheme of understanding and operation, nor is it a more radical way of uncritical toleration. Rather it is an offering of self to a narrative and a Person. The narrative unfolds a process which hinges upon identity being focussed in the prayer "not my will, but Thine, be done.". These are the words that begin the story of Jesus, from Mary's lips (Luke 1[38]), and complete it in Gethsemane (Luke 22[42]). The doctrines and creeds of the church highlight the features of this narrative, within which fleshly life and the new life of eternity are joined through an act of crucifixion: sacrifice of self in recognition of the absolute limitations of the flesh and yet an acknowledgement of the absolute freedom of the body touched by eternity. This theology is not aimed at the secular "in order to" – which is about construction of public space and personal identity as measurable achievement. Rather it recognises the key offering of self "for the sake of": the great emphasis of the life of Jesus, especially in Holy Week[1]. This is not the rational calculation associated with organised religion, evidenced in the words of Caiaphas, "it is better for one man to die for the sake of the people" (John 11[50]) i.e. *in order to* save the people. Rather it provokes an outcome which is beyond neat explanation or understanding, in the bursting forth of new life from the tomb "for the sake of" the salvation of the world – most powerfully illustrated at Pentecost with the outpouring of the One Spirit in a multitude of different and competing tongues.

There is a temptation in the church to offer "normalisation" under the banner "Be Nice."[2] Church presents as a community of consensus and conformity – a clear measure for membership and for those outside. Doctrine needs to be clear and comprehensible to reinforce this stance. This, in fact, represents the security-seeking legalism of established religion which Jesus challenged so directly.

The formational basis of the church is a creed: a narrative which calls for engagement with a representative person and a definitive process. The power of narrative is both its openness to interpretation, and its ability to hold in tension the complexities of consensus and conflict. With fraction and self sacrifice at the heart of the narrative, there is an inbuilt guard against a simple triumphalism which offers anything like a complete package of belief and behaviour. Rather the formational crux of sacrifice, fraction, owning incompleteness and seeing, but through a glass darkly, guarantees a community united in the deeper undercurrents of a common life-giving spirit, rather than through measurable marks of conformity. There needs to be space for nonconformity within the dynamics of Christian community: not to offer uncritical worship of a god of Toleration, but to ensure that obedience to the Person of the Master and to the process of the master narrative calls every participant to live by the humility of confessing failings (the mote in one's own eye), and thus to call others into an uneven, rough edged conformity. High ideals will still be central, but as marks for negotiating the complexities of conformity and nonconformity, as a continuing dynamic – rather than seeking to rest in what can appear to be some kind of final solution[3].

In this sense Christian communities are called to be laboratories of difference and dialogue, exploring the conflicts within each person, as well as those between people and groups. The tendency to a simplified outward conformity may provide a degree of comfort, but it will fail to engage with the call to a deeper and more eternal maturity that emerges from continuing discernment of the underlying currents of spiritual life – a single stream enervating a bewildering variety of manifestations, many of which seem to focus around basic binary oppositions such as those between light and dark, male and female, right and wrong. In fact the path towards graciousness as revealed in the Father is travelled through faith in grasping the good enough, which keeps us open to new learning and the reality of a continuing pruning of our achievements. The deepest dependency needs to be upon the single source of life, the Holy Spirit, rather than upon particular manifestations and moments in human history.

This paradox of purpose and yet provisionality is held by the focussing narrative of a Person, and a process of sacrifice – offering "on behalf of" others and "on behalf of" that Other who is perfection and also parent: Our Father.

This approach to community is an essential context for the continual testing, refining and nourishment of private faith, and provides a model of connection and catholicity which equips participants to have the insight and courage to offer pastoral and prophetic words and signs (sacraments) to act as light and leaven to enable the emergence of love in human hearts within the various associations formed as part of the work of constructing that second environment of meaning and direction that enables the creation of public space.

The conflict between conformity and non-conformity can be creatively challenging and refining of both positions and enables the emergence of transcendence through the Pentecost principle of a radical pluriformity held in a common source and goal. The outpouring of new life includes an element of unpredictability (hence the "newness") which must add to, and deepen appreciation of, the ultimate. There can never be a one-dimensional account of truth, only a living engagement – which is why the courage to ask questions and explore narrative is so important to purge people of mere "opinions." Formation occurs through participation in a community operating around these principles. There is a profound difference between "possessing the truth," which is not possible, and "knowing the truth"[4], which involves dynamic engagement with a living and life-giving force. J S Mill recognised that in the operation of a healthy political order there needed to be a party of order and a party of reform[5]. This is a secularised version of Augustine's insight that the church will always be a corpus permixtum.

In such a mixed but focussed community, committed to one Person and the narrative of the process He manifests, sovereignty is not located in the aggregation of individual wills, nor in an intellectualised reason (presupposing some objectivity and completion), rather it is located in the underlying spirit which gives life in all its complexities, and offers a means of engagement that can be both purifying and connecting with a richer reality. This relativizes all other attempts to claim sovereignty. The priority of prayerful reflection, shaping by sacramental signs and scriptural interpretation, and humble self-giving service will enable communities of Christian formation to offer example and resource to other human associations and their individual members – especially in highlighting the possibilities of a transforming transcendence of particularity.

This Christian making of community will not provide answers or certainty in relation to the practical problems of constructing public space – but by manifesting the sheer joy of living together with the challenging (and often tragic) realities of pluralism and apparently incompatible differences, there is a formational witness of the absolute priority which needs to be given to owning our need of the presence of others within a narrative rooted in the deep truth of Otherness as the energy of life.

The root of this approach is summarised by the word "ethos." The classic example is the speech by Pericles to the Athenians following defeat and the loss of fighting men[6]. In his speech Pericles does not offer an explanation, or a programme to put things right in an immediate or conclusive way. Rather he recalls the glory of the past, as inspiration and energy for the future. There is an ethos which embraces Athens, her history, her present context and her future. People should be proud to be part of this ethos, which gives life, hope and a perspective to put the present in context.

The same process is highlighted in the liturgy of the Christian community where remembering, reflecting and thus trusting in the future is focussed upon the definitive person of Jesus the Christ, the witness of His followers, and the enduring values and goals of His Kingdom. This is a wisdom which transcends the "evidence" of immediate experience. It has a power which is not dependent upon intellectual understanding, but upon participation in the life of the community which is ever forming around the challenge and comfort of such "good news." Broad invitations to love God and to love neighbour are beyond neat definition, but offer an engagement with others and otherness that can provide shape and direction to human being. Ethos depends upon faith: it involves intellectual understanding, and emotional experience, but transcends both. It is the root of the wager to live "on behalf of" someone and something greater than the self. Ethos enables different interpretations and experiences to find a common energy and direction, without negotiating a tangible reconciliation – since each perspective and priority is raised into something more embracing, mysterious but totally real.

To create and sustain this "ethos" liturgy needs to ensure a remembering and a reflection based upon the person of Jesus the Christ, the witness of His followers, but also the present concerns of disciples and the world in which we are set. Past, present and future interact – not just in a narrow church, institutional perspective – but as the essential ingredients of a Kingdom of Heaven-on-earth agenda. At present this wider experience, anxiety and hopefulness is only represented through the headlines of intercessory prayers and sermon illustrations. There is an urgent need for the widest range of contemporary experiences and the sharpest analyses seeking understanding and assessment to be embraced more robustly into the dynamics of the liturgy and the lived-out witness of the Christian community. Otherwise its life will collapse into self-referencing survival and the temptation to judge "the world" from afar – rather than to participate in its transformation through faith in the possibilities of Heaven-on-Earth. Jesus was always proceeding on to the next village.

The inner life of reflection depends upon this broad cocktail of ingredients if it is to enable the bringing to birth of new life that is good news for the purposes of creation and its salvation. The fact that it is rooted in parable and paradox enables both conflict (for example Jesus' criticism of the Pharisees for their excessive legalism) and consensus (His agreement with them on the centrality of Law). While it is important to seek clearer intellectual understanding of such issues, and the place of individual rights and uniqueness within such tensions, there is a recognition of continuing complexity and incompletion, and yet a way of coping by the construction of public space around a community of faith and an ethos which transcends the present by its recognition of determinative markers from the past, and aspirations for the future.

A powerful illustration of this process of constructing community in a public place around a defining Person is the story of the walk to Emmaus (Luke 24[13-35]). Conversation, involving "an other" explores challenging experiences, problems not easily resolvable by intellectual understanding, division between people. The Person who provides a reference point indicates an ethos and direction from the past (held in definitive texts) and narratives unveiling hope for the future. All these ingredients remain incomplete when this newly formed and extended community assembles around a table to share bread. Suddenly the searching disciples are embraced in a much more radical process, the transformation of Resurrection, of new life emerging from fragments of experience and understanding held by reference to a Person and a process. In this public arena, private faith is drawn into something life-giving that can construct a richer web of relationships and future perspective than would be possible from any of the individual resources in the initial presentation. This is not evolution, the grasping of the next stage in an incremental progression of learning and control – rather this process is one of emanation: something more of the deeper current of spiritual life is unveiled and appropriated, to give a common ethos and direction in the midst of unresolved differences and incomplete perspectives. Laws are important, but grace provides a much richer form of existence – the seed of beauty and truth that is manifest in history, in the present, in future hopes, yet which is capable of helping us see and trust in so much more. The means of this mystery becoming manifest are located in the construction of public space through community – comprising the interaction not of individuals, but of the associations which give their lives meaning and direction. The church can never accept a place in society simply as one association among many: a charter to practice a "private" faith in circumscribed conditions. The charter of the church is to model and enact the creation of community from the interaction of the stories, experiences, fears, failures and hopes of all the associations within which human life is being formed. Salvation is offered to the whole of creation, and the church can only be true to this gospel if it claims potential engagement with every attempt to construct public space – not to provide answers, but to offer essential ingredients and an ethos which can enable the potential in human being to flourish most fruitfully.

This contribution to the creation of public space will always be critical. Not because the church knows best (she does not!), but because Christians endeavour to love not their neighbour, but what their neighbour is not (yet), just as there is a call not to love self, but what self is not (yet). Prophecy is rootedness in the ethos that remembers signs of God's transforming power for goodness and new life, and thereby kindles a faith in the continuing miracle of such transformation, recognising that the path is often one of struggle and costly crucifixion.

The Church of England still has a unique opportunity to enable interaction between the different associations and interest groups that constitute society and contribute to the construction of the "second environment" in which life unfolds. The liturgy remains a key tool, but the challenge is how this instrument focussed upon a Person and a process might best act as leaven and light – particularly in a culture where "normalisation" implies the viability of a more individual, disconnected understanding of reality. The strategy coheres around three interrelated activities, prayer, conversation, and the bringing to birth of new life – the practice that defines formation.

CHAPTER 11

The End of Democracy:
The Beginning of Freedom

One of the great phrases of the first decade of the twenty-first century in the west is the expression "taking things forward." There is an obsession with the next steps on the path of progress. Faith is rooted in the evolutionary theory of Charles Darwin. There is no longer term vision for the future, a fuller, more fleshed-out teleology: such big pictures command little attention to generations locked into the present tense and its immediate evolution. The small scale of the perspective makes it more credible to believe that such progress is both achievable and manageable.

Similarly, there is very little interest in the past – at least as an ostensible resource for understanding and shaping the present. There may be recognition of the very immediate history, but otherwise confidence (faith) is located in the evidentially based skills of the human sciences for interpreting the present and its realisable potential. The enduring fascination with heritage (now reduced to the realms of television and tourism) and the continuing political dominance of the factors around the aspirations of Empire, should sound as clear warnings that past and future are, in fact, much more powerful forces in contemporary societies – whatever the apparent prevalence of the concentration upon "moving forward."

There are three basic ingredients to this controlled restlessness. One is the presupposition of atomised individualism. The basic unit of reality is each unique, precious person, with their personal rights. The art of government is to enable as much freedom as possible, while holding the ring in a minimalist way in order to prevent harm to the vulnerable, and in order to ensure adequate systems to organise a flow of goods and services to support this culture of freedom.

The second ingredient of such controlled restlessness is an emphasis upon the sheer superabundance of energy and creativity that seems to be capable of emerging from humankind. The revolution crystallised by the Romantic Movement was to locate meaning and identity in the freely chosen words and actions that expressed the integrity and essence of the person. The very uniqueness of each expression was a mark of their value, and of the fulfilment of the person choosing and willing to exercise such creativity[1].

The third element of this controlled restlessness is the continuing recognition of the role of expertise – to interpret and shape human life in a way that provides both space for freedom with creativity, and which protects the accumulated insights of wisdom and skilled analysis. There is general recognition that restlessness needs some kind of control, alongside the opportunity for creativity, located primarily in the unique preciousness of the individual. Some later exponents of Romanticism such as Fichte, called for a more corporate approach to creativity[2], but the forces of capitalism have ensured that even the nationalisms of democratic states take second place in everyday life to the forces of fashion and the exercise of individual choice in the global marketplace.

Since the industrial revolution the churches have tended to conform to these patterns. Liberal democracy has been adapted into ecclesiastical polities, putting the individual believer in a prime role as a unique subject. Church life tends to be a dynamic between service and mission. Service offers pastoral support and encouragement in the development of individual creativities, and helps to pick up the pieces when things go wrong. Hence the expanding horizon for positive pastoral care for the casualties of the collapse of family life, and the debates about the potential creativity of a whole range of lifestyles. Priests are rebranded as Servant Leaders: church buildings find a new lease of life by providing space for community and caring activities: "love" is the word which provides energy and an apologetic. The main aim is to help people find "the way forward" on their own particular journey.

At the same time there is a powerful instinct for mission in terms of a unifying message and modelling of behaviour alongside the importance of legitimate expertise. There is a stream of increasing fundamentalism about moral teaching, the centrality of dogma and the importance of a common framework for worship. Human freedom and creativity needs authoritative interpretation and guidance. Grace depends upon Law as one of the foundational factors in human being. There is even sign of a shift from the call for disciplined individual lives towards the establishment of disciplined communities – a distinctiveness preserved by degrees of separation from other lifestyles on offer.

While it is inevitable that the church should unfold her life within the contours of the culture in which she is set – hence the common interplay between grace/freedom and law/ management by expertise, all based upon a faith in the individual as the focus of meaning and the test of authenticity – nonetheless, there is something in the history and in the future of the church which needs to be reclaimed. This is something which coheres with the prevalence of a desire for heritage and the fascination with Empire[3].

This currently much neglected element is that of settlement. The parochial system, with the location of a church in a specific community, is a powerful sign that the dynamic between mission and service, between law and grace, between control and freedom, is always enacted within a particular place[4]. The undercurrent of divine purpose emerging into its human being as the spirit of Holiness and new life is always incarnated: made flesh in particular persons in particular places. Within the context of enfleshment the spirit of creativity, and the spirit equally of discipline, emerges and is embodied: in individuals, in their associations, and in the interplay between them. Human being is always bounded by limitation, yet hopeful of eternity. The particularity of being placed puts an accent upon history, especially its more recent manifestation as "heritage." Knowledge of roots gives clues to the meaning and purpose of life, and criteria by which to judge the sources of good fruits and bad ones. According to Arendt "mortals need this touchstone of permanence."[5]

Awareness of being placed also provides a basis for the instinct in human hearts for ultimate fulfilment, often expressed in earthly forms through the political notion of Empire. In the Book of Revelation there is a graphic illustration of the call to acknowledge a king and a kingdom being transformed into an eternity of glory and catholic comprehensiveness. All individuality is subsumed in an all embracing oneness with others and with the Glory of God – in worship.

In this sense of providing a settlement in various places, the church offers herself as a resource to individuals and associations, in which the inevitable dynamic between freedom and order, grace and law, can be literally earthed – tested, fragmented, re-membered: so that a process of pruning and fruiting, held up in a person crucified and resurrected, can be a model – not for conformity, but as a reference point for decisions, mistakes and successes, to be worked around. Whatever the trends, the fashions in faith, in identity, or in consumption, the uneven interplay of the forces that constitute this "controlled restlessness" through which mature human being unfolds, can be ever affirmed, challenged, changed and redirected. Not simply in a manner which best "takes things forward": but in a much more radical sense of offering the perspectives of history and ultimate hope, past and future: so that the search for identity and fulfilment is always located in the realities of what seems to be, what might be immediately possible – as part of owning what has been given, and what is ultimately on offer.

Settlement makes every private faith an ingredient in a realistic construction of public space. Incarnation is the principle which enables atonement: the miracle of incomplete, separated and sinful persons being cleansed, renewed and remade into a single body by incorporation into the life and death and resurrection of a Person – Jesus the Christ. The narrative of His story opens up a process to refine and rightly direct practice, and provide a sounding board for reflection on the currents of the inner life which can engender energy and direction for those who learn to conform to its flow. The church is not charged with the construction of public space. Rather the church has a particular contribution by being a settler: simply saying, whatever the dynamics in operation at this moment to try to create that second environment, the church is present: settled, rooted, connected with the context within which these dynamics are being played out. This includes chaplaincy to sectors not just geographic parish ministry. As a settlement the Christian community emphasises the centrality of place (context), for spirit to be made flesh (incarnation), requiring refinement (atonement) and a site of lively engagement and exploration for all the constituent parts. In this sense of "settlement" the church is able to embrace as constituent parts both unique and precious individuals, and all manner of associations. Each part has an instinct for heritage and an instinct for empire. Each is aware of the need to live by going forward, but requires skills and tools to take such steps with a sense of continuity, coherence and increasing closeness to the full fruition of the dreams and desires which provide energy and aspiration to human hearts. The web of relationships through which these dynamics are unfolded are modelled within the ecclesial association which presents as church, but only by way of fallible illustration, partialness and encouragement. Anything more conclusive or definitive would have become "God" rather than a discipling of His call to participate in the unfolding creation of new life. Thus, "the performance of a system is not the sum of the performances of the various parts, but the product of their interactions"[6].

There is space for toleration – but never as an ultimate. Nor can the aggregation of individual choices be a guarantee of truth or the rightness of the way forward. Liberal democracy as a method and as a goal is proving to be increasingly bankrupt. These basic incompatibilities were recognised by Plato in the Republic[7]. The worship of liberty is incompatible with the worship of ordering by either the will of the majority or by those whose messianic manipulation seems to provide sense and direction.

To be properly inclusive of individual uniqueness, the key formational roles of a myriad of associations, and the central requirement of human being for there to be a creative play between freedom and order, grace and law – there needs to be a way of modelling community that has porous boundaries, a humility about the ever present need for fraction and re-membering in the construction of a second environment, and a central place for a Person representative of, and infusing life into, every human being. His story provides material for the interpretation of all other narratives, against the interplay of freedom and order, fraction and community – the technical term is the unfolding of Holy Communion. This is not simply a sign of the church: rather it is the sign of the presence of the church as the body of Christ, the foretaste of the Kingdom of God, available to be accessed through inner reflection on the deepest currents of creativity and the more immediate experiences of survival and short term aspiration for "moving forward."

Liberal democracy continues to be the cause of conflict, oppression, manipulation- the effacing of the image of God as creativity and uniqueness in each human person and association. On its own it creates an environment ripe for conquest by the totalitarianism of celebrity and hopes which seem manageable through the mechanisms of nationalism and empire. Worship of the god of Toleration provides uncritical public space for forces of demonic fundamentalism to seize or manipulate the sheer fluidity of post modern space, and simply magnify what is already present: boredom, emptiness and an unsatisfiable desire for consumer goods and experiences.

The goodness within liberal democracy needs to be rooted in the settlement which the church alone offers: the reality of placedness, diversity, conflict yet desire for consensus, creativity generally outworking as incoherence. All this is located within the sign of a community calling associations and individuals to taste, test and ever refashion freedom and order through the mortality and vulnerability of fleshliness and the eternal and completeness of purifying spirit: the process of death and resurrection in the Person of Jesus the Christ.

This is an approach accessed by habitus – an ethos that embraces and holds faith through committed practice, while not seeking full intellectual comprehension as a necessary starting point. Human life is a process of formation through undulation – lows and highs, deaths and resurrections. Obsession with the myth of "understanding" and of measurable outcomes to take things forward, offers voters an unreal choice, and serves to keep power safely in the hands of those who have constructed a monopoly of holding and negotiating the big picture – which is accessed through the manipulation of fashion and the fulfilments demanded by private faith.

To accept the fact of settlement as a core to human experience is to face the need for sacrifice of self to enable openness to the new possibilities that can be created by the confluence of difference and a stronger commitment to explore potential through faith in a deeper, common undercurrent and final fulfilment. This is the seed of private faith becoming a public energy for the construction of a second environment which is always subject to critique and challenge, fraction and fallenness, while being, nonetheless, empowered to reshape and regrow. This public creativity will operate through manageable, located units, aspiring to owning interpenetration with other associations in a common current of spiritual energy.

Liberal Democracy, especially with the collapse of rooted connection through political parties, does not invite serious engagement with the inner life – either of individuals or of institutions. Rather there is an appeal for occasional acts of support (via the ballot box) and general consensus towards policy development. Otherwise the presupposition is that private life will be free to be practiced according to personal faith and principles, with the operation of liberal democracy simply providing a mechanism for occasional negotiation of the minimalist framework that enables coherence and connection where necessary. The prevalence of deep undercurrents of nationalism, and the frantic creation of communities of commitment around celebrities and sports stars/teams, indicates that basic human aspirations are finding no outlet in terms of public ritual and the trappings of more intimate identity-in-common. The inner life has been privatised, to give those who wield social and economic influence a monopoly of power in terms of the construction of public space which is "light" in its demands, generous in giving scope for difference, and apparently essential to providing the right conditions for individual flourishing.

In fact liberal democracy appeals to people across cultures not because it represents the face of a crude capitalism that mercilessly exploits individual isolation and insecurity by ever shifting the fashions which indicate the marks of acceptable identity. Rather it appeals to a deeper instinct in the human heart – for connection, and something more complete, more coherent and more expressive of the ultimate in terms of goodness, grace, beauty and harmony. This agenda is left to the market forces of artistic creativity within contemporary liberal democracies, particularly through the fashions of popular culture. In fact it requires much more focussed expression and enactment: rooted clearly in the past, and in the aspiration of the heart for future perfection. These instincts are seeking for some kind of Holy Communion – realistic about the present, critical but appreciative of the past , and hope-ful about the future – operating through marks that acknowledge the complexities of the narratives of life through personhood, through associations, through processes, and through the interplay of prayerful reflection and provisional practice. The centrality of humility, being open to correction and pruning, the miracle of fraction yielding new beginning and the indestructibility of hope in the human heart. These are the signs illuminated in the representative Person of Jesus the Christ, exemplified in the workings of a church deployed through the incarnation of settlement, and inviting of various degrees of participation from those who take time to discern the deeper currents of spiritual flow which bring forth life, new life and the embracingness of a Heavenly Kingdom (Atonement). There needs to be a shift from aiming to accelerate "the way forward" towards deepening engagement with what was, and is, and is to be. This kind of placed participation is the bedrock of what the early church called koinonia.

With its emphasis upon the "reign of God" Christianity established and settled in each community an understanding of sovereignty which was an inversion of the normal symbols of power, freedom and order. The royal title of the incarnate One was inscribed on a cross. This marked the creation of a new type of social organisation – the church: "not based on kin or interest or law or place or national identity – but based on faith." [8] This is the implication of St Paul's revolutionary pronouncement in Galatians that in Christ there is neither Jew nor Greek, slave nor free, male nor female (Galatians 3[28]). There is no permanent (ultimate) city on earth, and thus Christians offer engagement with a community which is a settlement of strangers – aliens in a foreign land: supporters yet re-makers of society and each of its citizens (1 Peter 2[13-17], I Timothy 2[1-2], Titus 3). Participation is rooted primarily in faith in God – a divine sovereignty creating and calling for perfection. Only secondarily and temporarily can there be faith in human construction of public space and a second environment. This will be always proleptic and preliminary, yet necessarily particular and grounded in the dynamics of accepting proximity as the basic place of engagement. Such is the element so dangerously absent from a culture based upon the worship of the god of Toleration, the mechanisms of liberal democracy and the atomised uniqueness of each individual. Settlement in the ultimacy of God needs to be made manifest in exploring the realities of human settlement – the fact of being located in relation to others. This dynamic needs to operate not simply through liberal democracy, but more significantly through the deeper realism of a greater interplay betweem conformity and non-conformity which produces freedom in all its fullness.

CHAPTER 12

Beyond the God of Toleration: the Christian Contribution

Characteristic of the Judaism from which Jesus the Christ came was a fierce monotheism. The story of the Jewish scriptures is that of the recurring temptation to worth-ship the Baals – localised dispersed sovereignty, compacted to give identity and security to particular peoples and contexts. In the story of Rachel fleeing her family home there is even recognition of family gods (Genesis 31[19]).

This emphasis upon the oneness of God, as Almighty and Eternal, Creator and Redeemer, is equally counter cultural in the world of liberal democracy and global capitalism. Witness to this single source of life and salvation tends to be temporised by accommodations to current philosophies and practices, as the making of Church almost always shows signs of being in the image of the political and cultural systems within which it is set.

These elements of convergence can provide points of connection, but risk undermining the radical challenge and invitation offered by the oneness of God revealed in the one Lord Jesus the Christ. The instinct to reach out to every person and place needs to be balanced by the sheer depth and integrity of the home base: the source emerges most clearly from the gifts through which it is offered: signs and stories (scriptures and creeds) water, bread and wine (sacraments) and an authoritative, representative ministry[1]: all earthed in the reality of settlement or being located in relation to others. This is the dynamic between the Son of Man and the Son of God.

The liberal, inclusive, outgoing Church, and the conserving, clarifying, compacted Church both depend on a common base: a base which offers transforming resources not simply for the construction of ecclesial space, but more profoundly, for the construction of public space in its largest manifestations. Liberal democratic culture is in urgent need of these resources if it is to survive the imploding tendencies implicit in Capitalism, or the totalising dangers of sofa-Messiahship calling out 'opinions' which seem ready to 'take things forward.'

What the Christian Gospel has to offer can be grouped under a number of headings.

First, aspects of faith. The natural human desire for success and assurance of its durability and appropriateness (the driver of fashion and sofa-Messiahship) needs to be balanced by an honest recognition of the reality of the tragic in human living. This is evident in the ever present gap between aspiration and delivery: the temptation to selfish pleasure and security at the expense of others: the sometimes wilful destructiveness of undisciplined instincts and the love of power. The tragedy of this tension between desire for the good; the potential, sometimes, to be 'good enough'; and the reality of, sometimes, failing disastrously and engendering destruction and evil, is held up with withering clarity in the sign of the cross. In this moment are made manifest political, religious and cultural choices, magnified by the democratic expression of the majority of the people, attempting to destroy the One whose story explores these tensions with clarity and challenge. The miracle of His life surviving death, and rising to inspire and inhabit others, speaks to the deepest aspirations of human hearts. Reality and hopefulness meet in the realm of crucifixion and resurrection. This instinct of faith needs a narrative to unlock the meaning of other narratives that have tended to become trapped within the limitations of private faith and self referencing support groups. Because this kind of faith is universal in human hearts, there needs to be a common way of enabling the exploration and expression of it – as a foundational ingredient to the forces deployed in the construction of public space. Apologetic and prophecy are both experiences of these deepest currents of spiritual life, and together can illuminate the coherence between the Christian calling and witness, and the ways in which the world might be most fruitfully pruned of destructiveness to enable the first signs of growth of a new earth, which is itself an image of a new heaven, an ultimacy for which the whole creation groans (Romans 8).

An important refinement is the dynamic of faith and forgiveness. This is the ability to allow new life to emerge from limitation and failure by letting go of security seeking absolutes and risking the diminution of the self as the beginning of receiving something new. There is an urgent need for forgiveness and self sacrifice to become recognisable elements of how the second environment is imagined and outlined. Similarly there is need for much more emphasis upon the artistic - the creative spirit through which the soul flourishes: probably best exemplified by Schiller's notion of play as an activity in which the normal rules and limitations of nature are transcended by the construction of another 'world' in which all kinds of perfections are possible[2]. The Christian Gospel encourages the courage to imagine and explore more perfect ways of relating and using creation – signs of transcendence that can give focus to attempts to deal with the seemingly harsher realities. This appeal to art and the spirituality of imagination is an important counter to the current scientific emphasise upon measurement, predictability and empiricism[3].

These aspects of faith require 'space' for reflection upon the signs of the times, the signs of the tradition (scripture, creeds, sacraments, authoritative ministry), and the scope for imagination and new beginnings. Such richer perspective often comes through a discipline of withdrawal, waiting and sometimes being in the wilderness. How can ecclesial and political life have faith enough to create such spaces and invite not just individuals, but associations and societies to take them seriously? In the nineteenth century there was a tradition of facing challenges such as cholera by a national day of prayer. Eventually scientists persuaded governments that a better response would be via a Royal Commission to develop the most effective response[4]. The pragmatic success in relation to cholera should not obscure the loss of a valuable element within the ecology of public life – for the people as much as for the politicians. Space for reflection requires places where the fruits of insights and inspiration gained can be shared and tested, not by instant telephone poll decisions, but by thoughtful discussion, debate and a willingness to explore difference creatively (seeking new life) rather than succumbing to the temptation to close things down into forms which seem to be more immediately manageable.

Thus the elements of 'faith' that the Christian Gospel might contribute to the formation of private faith and public space, need congenial structures through which they can be held up, engaged with and pursued. The narrowly ecclesial structures which gather Christians for worship too easily become 'private' spaces for self referencing groups who then offer pastoral care to those struggling in the wider world. Love as pastoral outreach becomes the currency of mission – to great effect. But what is so often lacking is space to craft a credible critique of contemporary society, and illustrative prophetic action in terms of distinctive behaviour and lifestyle. To honour our worship of the Father in Heaven whose will is to be done on earth (not just in the Church) requires this imbalance to be addressed – in terms of the style and content of worship, outreach and overt engagement with the big picture. At present millions of God's children fall outside the scope of the arenas of reflection, discussion and responsive action.

Fruitful study might be made of the effectiveness of the Early Church in crafting advice about very specific behaviour for particular contexts, including style of dress, types of diet, appropriate employment choices and approaches to family responsibilities. Of especial significance was the totally counter cultural emphasis in the Graeco-Roman world upon sexual purity. These disciplines of behaviour provided light and leaven in terms of indicating values and views that others who stopped to reflect seriously about their deepest instincts and institutions were able to recognise. Public behaviour of private individuals provided signs of that deeper current of spiritual life ever offered to refine and refocus human beings in its current state of limitation and pull towards selfish satisfaction and survival. Such witness makes manifest the nature of Christian 'settlement': the placedness of the spirit of eternity.

Another area of modelling creative behaviour is that of exploring how distinctive groups and associations can find common roots in the forces of creation while owning the reality of differences, darkness and a desire to judge others more conclusively. The emphasis upon relationship with a Person, engagement with a process, through prayerful reflection and risk taking practice for-the-sake-of-the-whole – all points towards the importance of ambiguity and the acceptance of ignorance alongside moments of illumination and inspiration. This mixture of humility and maturity could provide an important corrective to a fairly militant empiricism measured by the fantasy of graphs of continuing improvement. The gospel calls for the creation of networks of solidarity formed on such a basis.

The god of Toleration is worshipped on the basis that 'yes is best'. 'No' should be minimised, since it restricts the freedom of individuals and hints at a negativity which often seems to be 'abusive' to the liberal democratic mind. By contrast, the Gospel of Jesus Christ not only affirms the oneness of God, who shall have no rivals (Exodus 20[3]), but further, makes clear that the fallen condition of humanity demands that the first and most important word is 'No'. The Ten Commandments are rooted in the necessity of this restrictive covenant, and the ministry of Jesus shows that the spiritual journey must begin by dealing with the temptations of self-concern – each needing to be answered with a 'No' (Luke 4[1-13]). The positiveness of the Lord's Prayer shows a marked contrast (Luke 11[1-4]), but is controlled by the unifying admission 'Our Father': a common source and goal of life.

At present the power of 'No' has been so circumscribed that only abuse of children and the freedom of others seem to warrant any kind of check or control. The Christian Gospel calls upon human kind to recognise that sin and failure are deep within human being, and thus the word of invitation to engagement with the deeper currents of life is 'Repent', i.e., say 'No' to what is most immediate in terms of instinct and opportunity – in order to find a richer, more fulfilling pathway – a 'Yes' to the oneness of God and the cleansing and salvation of creation.

The resistance of a liberal democratic culture to any suggestion of giving priority to the word 'No' is a mark of the challenge to be faced in casting down the god of Toleration and inviting people to meet Jesus the Christ, risen from the dead. In fact this challenge is an invitation to dialogue, within churches and within society, through a series of interconnected, differentiated spaces where various kinds of public faith can be contested and focussed. Christian churches are challenged to provide models, leaven and light for engagement beyond their own borders, and a priority for the fundamental formational spaces of family, neighbourhood, nation: the places of settlement within which choices about life and its direction need to be made[5]. The big pictures to which hearts aspire (love

God – the whole project: love neighbours – the needy and the stranger) need focussing and expressing.

The key tools for this task are the God-given signs of sacraments, credal and scriptural narratives and authoritative leadership which together connect past, present, and future possibility. They provide ingredients for the making of holy communion – through enabling the owning of limitation and of sin; the offering of the self to be associated with sacrifice and fraction; and the engagement with an ethos which holds and divides, while leaving issues of precise understanding and action frustratingly, and yet life givingly, open. However, within the sphere of privatised expression, christianity has tended to concentrate upon encouraging individual conversion, deepening in the faith, and subsequent witness and invitation to others. The Alpha phenomenon would be an example of the success and appropriateness of this strategy – which has clear provenance in the New Testament. A second emphasis is that devoted to refining the institutional arrangements and presentation of the Christian faith – the development of people, buildings and systems of organisation.

Alongside these essentially internal expressions of the faith, it is vital to recognise that the power of the mission of Jesus Christ, and of St Paul, in laying the foundations of a public faith, depended upon offering something that was distinctive and unique: the forgiveness of sins and the possibility of eternal life. Individual conversion and development, alongside the necessary organisational shaping and structures were only part of this more primary operation.

In a time of hyper concern about professionalisation, standards and benchmarks, it is imperative for the Christian Church to keep her primary focus upon the foundational spiritual mandate to expose and confront the choices between good and evil, and to offer resources of holiness and wholeness, manifested in Jesus Christ and freely outpoured to all who would receive the abundance of blessing God offers for the fulfilment of His creatures. This invitation and transaction begins with the challenge of 'Repent': say 'No' to immediate selfish and sensuous desires, for the sake of opening up richer expectations and blessings – the life of the Kingdom, incorporation into the Body of Christ. Society and each of its members must be challenged to acknowledge the primary state of incompletion, and the yearnings of the human heart for fulfilment beyond what can be seen or experienced more immediately. Hence Augustine's famous dictum: 'Our hearts are restless till they find their rest in you'. Here God is the source and the completion of every intimation in the human heart for goodness, beauty, justice and peace.

In this sense Christianity does not provide an alternative, superior system – rather it offers an essential resource to all attempts to understand and shape human life for the best. The Christian Gospel is absolute, but not universalist: there will be many ways of appropriating the deep truth which faith in Jesus Christ inspires. Hence the salvation of the world is not offered simply through membership of the Church focussed in a particular type of conformity. Rather salvation springs from a dynamic engagement with hope in the human heart, sometimes focussed in a more concentrated manner through membership of a Church, sometimes experienced through interaction with the values, lifestyles and intellectual formulations of Christian witness. There are various forms of settlement offering tasting and testing places, while seeking a broader connectivity too. Faith in Jesus Christ provides light and leaven, often offered through interaction with small associations or groups. The tendency to see religion in more inclusive, macro terms, such as the integrative element in society (Durkheim) or the expression of ultimate meaning (Berger: Bellah: Parsons), does not easily apply to Christianity.[6] The particularity of a cross, and the focus of expression through settlement offers a more subtle influence, operating through the dynamic of a deep interpenetration of the Holy Spirit, and a range of often apparently disconnected manifestations. It is in this sense that Christianity is always a 'faith' – a hope in things as yet unseen, yet intimated in the aspirations of the heart.

As the letter of James makes clear, such faith is only effective when manifested in practice, that is, made incarnate, not simply within the workings of Church institutions, but primarily through interaction with the wider ebb and flow of human experience and struggle. The measure of the truth will be the points of interaction with other systems in the organisation of human being: lifestyle witness and intellectual apologetic are not simply for the sake of church members – rather these expressions of the Gospel are to be tested, refined and renewed through robust interaction with others. Truth in the deep connectivity of a common spirit and the power of sacrifice to move the human soul, gives confidence to Christians to walk this way of the cross.

To make this kind of witness the Church needs coherence and consistency in its practice and in its proclamation. Any attempt to embrace manifestly different values and practices provides a code for confusion and an undermining of credibility. Historically difference has been handled by hierarchy and segmentation: focussed on different models of settlement. Thus the monastic movement offered a particularly intense and detailed focus upon purity of practice: clergy and laity existed in other modes of settlement. This kind of scheme is realistic about the importance of boundaries and clarity, the sheer variety of human being, and the value of different types of practice and aspiration. Nonetheless, a common focus on a Person and a process provided an essential connection and a rooting in the spirit of life seeking fulfilment. The modern tendency of the Church to 'level down' and not distinguish between degrees of intensity and achievement has undermined a delicate ecology which provided a far richer and more accessible witness and invitation to all the other approaches human beings invent to hold and handle their lives.[7] The refining of Christian witness, the recognition of those called to embrace ideals in the most rigorous manner, and the permission to enable a whole complex of alternative approaches is an urgent task. The forces of fashion imply particular paths as being appropriate for our times – a good example would be the exponential growth of Pentecostalism[8]. The subtle variations Jesus established through his small core groups, then the twelve, then the seventy-two, then other local settlements, points towards a much richer ecology within which faith can be called out and flourish. The expressive manifestation of this holding of complexity and common potential is that of table fellowship: the sharing of the means of life by diverse associations of people. Preparation by means of purification and then participation in conversation around sharing food and drink express the miracle of baptism and holy communion. Sacred signs and moments of settlement, solidarity and the seeking together of a greater salvation combine to provide structure and shaping that can connect diversity and cohesion in a dynamic and life-enhancing way.

In a world increasingly shaped by the totalising monopolies of liberal democracy, the bureaucratic state, academic education and positivistic science, the Christian Gospel calls for a more complex, uneven approach – owning unknowing and apparent incompatibilities alongside signs of seeing, harmony and justice. It is in the interplay of these two poles, not in their apparent resolution through human systems and constructs, that truth is explored and experienced. Faith calls out a journey into the unknown, confident that the love and light tasted and glimpsed, despite frightening evidence of contrary forces, can triumph in a richer and more ultimate manner: in the aspiration of the heart for the highest heaven. In Christian terms: the desire for resurrection from the deadness of atomised human being is the elemental energy of the soul that needs both the challenge and the encouragement of the Gospel of the Kingdom. Love promises to make human beings better than we might be, on a path to growth and fulfilment. The god of Toleration needs to be challenged by a God of such transforming love: manifested not through simple majority opinions, but through the effects of leaven and light on a creation pregnant with fulfilling potential, but deeply liable to the kind of short sighted, selfish satisfactions which stunt and damage what might be.

Besides encouraging an appropriate witness and leavening from individuals and associations, and their interplay with other forces in society, the time may have arrived at the beginning of the twenty first century for Christian churches to consider the possibility of cooperating with other faith groups to make a more focussed contribution to political life. As democracy has been extended to enable more participative political processes, energy and identity has tended to find focus in a clearer recognition of particular challenges and goals – in the later twentieth century the issue of equality, which gave grounding to socialist and welfare aspirations, and the issue of individual authority over moral and economic behaviour which gave impetus to neo-conservative politics.

In a new century where both of these political philosophies are struggling with the incoherence engendered by a common faith in secular liberal humanism, it may be important for Christians and those of other monotheistic faiths to explore how best to offer an alternative – not only in terms of personal values and identity, but equally important, in terms of social values and political organisation. God has provided in Jesus Christ resources richer and more potent than any human systems of reasoned aspiration and organisation. There may be a case for Christian churches to take a lead in the formation of a "faith movement" within democratic cultures, appealing to electorates on the basis of some of the vision and values outlined in these chapters, and explored by many contemporary Christian thinkers[10] and thus providing the possibility of a genuinely different political programme. Such a strategy would be a clear acknowledgement of the need to challenge the growing (and destructive) hegemony of secular liberal humanism, and a recognition of the responsibilities incumbent upon all whose faith is essentially a commitment to a universal, public "better way": the path to salvation. Some of the most creative and constructive work in this area is being pioneered by Pope Benedict XVI.[11]

Similarly, the time may have arrived for faith communities to develop an alternative to a media culture which is an equally uncritical champion of secularised liberal humanism with all its attendant contradictions and fake promises.

There are key issues of perspective, promise and performance. In each area the Christian gospel provides unique insights and agendas, often offering emphases that are closer to the concerns and values of other faith communities than those of a liberal bourgeois intelligentsia and its many creations of fashion, production and consumption.

However, these reflections point beyond the deliberate suggestiveness of this initial essay to more concrete possibilities. That urgent work needs further reflection and clarification.

Endnotes

Introduction

1. Havel, V (1985) *Politics and Conscience*: Salisbury Review, p.34.
2. Parsons, T (1960) *Structures and Processes in Modern Societies*: Free Press, p.134.
   Luckman, T (1967) *The Invisible Religion*: Macmillan, p.103.
   Boeve, L (2003) *Interrupting Tradition*: Peeters Part 1
3. Friedman, M (1962) *Capitalism and Freedom*: University of Chicago Press, p.13-15.
4. Hovey, C (2008) *Neitzsche and Theology*: T & T Clark, p85.
5. Hill, MA (Ed) (1979) *Hannah Arendt: The Recovery of the Public World*: St Martin's Press, p.233.
6. Davie, G (1994) *Religion in Britain since 1945: Believing without Belonging*: Backwell.
7. Berger, P (1967) *The Sacred Canopy: Elements of a Sociological Theory of Religion*: Doubleday, p.133.
   Bellah, R (1970) *Beyond Belief: Essays on Religion in a Post-Traditional World*: Harper and Row, p.43.
8. Hardy, DW (2001) *Finding the Church*: SCM, p.37-38.
9. Holland, HS, *Faith* in Gore C (1980) *Lux Mundi*: John Murray, p.8.

CHAPTER 1 - The Shape of Public Space

1. Herft, R (2008) *Lambeth Indaba: The Lambeth Conference*
2. Cassirer, E (1950) *The Problem of Knowledge*: Yale University Press, p.3.
3. Hovey, C (2008) *Nietzsche and Theology*: T & T Clark, p.83.
   Rowland, T (2003) *Culture and the Thomist Tradition*: Routledge, pxii.
4. Elliot, TS (1936) *Essays Ancient and Modern*: Harcourt Brace, p.128.

CHAPTER 2 - Embracing Sovereignty with Integrity

1. Mason, R (1994) *Cambridge Minds*: CUP, p.186.
2. Temple, W (1942) *Christianity and Social Order*: Penguin, p.31-32.

3. Lawson, P *English Pluralism* in Navari C (Ed) (1996) *British Politics and the Spirit of the Age*: Keele University Press, p68-69
    Schindler, J H (Ed) (2008) *Christianity and Civic Society*: Lexington

4. Putnam, D (2000) *Bowling Alone: the Collapse and Revival of American Community*: Simon and Schuster.

5. Redfern, A (1999) *Ministry and Priesthood*: DLT.

CHAPTER 3 - Environmental Choices

1. Hinchman, GP & SK (1994) *Politics as Culture in Hannah Arendt*: State University of New York Press, p.181.

CHAPTER 4 - The Art of Association

1. Villa, DR (1999) *Politics, Philosophy, Terror*: Princetown University Press, p.93.

2. *Ibid.*, p.141.

CHAPTER 5 - The Bankruptcy of Democracy

1. Fukuyama, F (1993) *The End of History and the Last Man*: Avon.

2. Bauckham, R (2002) *God and the Crises of Freedom: Biblical Contemporary Perspectives*: John Knox Press, pp.183-193.
    Williams, H, Sullivan D, Matthews G (1997) *Francis Fukuyama and the End of History*: Cardiff University Press.

3. Beyer, P (1994) *Religion and Globalisation*: Sage, p.105.

4. Cavanaugh, W (2008) *Being Consumed*: Eerdmans, pp.15-32.

5. Edelman Trust Barometer 2007.

6. Kitto, HDF (1962) *The Greeks*: Penguin, p78.

7. Isaac, J (1998) *Democracy in Dark Times*: Cornell University Press, p.32.

8. Habermas, J (1989) *The Structural Transformation of the Public Sphere*, MIT.

9. Arendt, H (1999) *Love and St Augustine*: University of Chicago Press, p.37.

10. Redfern, A (2004) *Being Anglican*: DLT.

CHAPTER 6 - Leadership and Followership

1. An example would be the narrow dependence upon the Archbishop of Canterbury at the 2008 Lambeth Conference in seeking to face the problems of the Anglican Communion.

2. Cassirer, E (1946) *The Myth of the State*: Yale University Press, p.131.
3. Turner, BS (1992) *Max Weber: From History to Modernity*: Routledge, p.116.
4. Stephens, RJ (2008) *The Fire Spreads*: Harvard University Press.
5. Meacham, S (1987) *Toynbee Hall and Social Reform 1880-1914: The Search for Community*: Yale University Press, p.2.
6. Benhabib, S (1996) *The Reluctant Modernism of Hannah Arendt*: Sage, p.13.

CHAPTER 7 - Inner Life and Its Outward Expression

1. Athanasiadis, H (2001) *George Grant and the Theology of the Cross*: University of Toronto Press, p.30.

CHAPTER 8 - Christians and the Construction of Public Space

1. Hare, J (1854) *The Mission of the Comforter*: Gould and Lincoln.
2. In modern terms this is the art of theological reflection. See Thompson, J (2008) *SCM Study Guide: Theological Reflection*. SCM.
3. Mendels, D (1999) *The Media Revolution of Early Christianity*: Eerdmans.
    Longenecker, B (2003) *The Lost Letters of Pergamum*: Grand Rapids, Baker.

CHAPTER 9 - The Organisation of Public Space

1. Headlam, S (1888) *The Laws of Eternal Life*: Verinder.

CHAPTER 10 - Identity and Community

1. Carr, AW (1992) *Tested by the Cross*: Fount.
2. Beyer, P (1994) *Religion and Globalisation*: Sage, p.102.
3. Andreski, S (1983) *Max Weber*: George Allen and Unwin, p.133.
4. Villa, D (2001) *Socratic Citizenship*: Princeton University Press, p.86.
5. Ibid, p.94.
6. Balot, R (2006) *Greek Political Thought*: Blackwell, p.59-60.

CHAPTER 11 - The End of Democracy: the Beginning of Freedom

1. Berlin, I (1996) *The Sense of Reality*: Pimlico, p.178.
    Bauman, Z (1993) *Postmodern Ethics*: Blackwell, p242
2. Berlin, *Ibid*, p.181.
3. Beyer, P (1994) *Religion and Globalisation*: Sage, p.91.

4. Redfern, A (2004) *Listening to the Anglican Tradition* in Martineau J, Francis LJ and Francis P (Eds) *Changing Rural Life*: Canterbury Press

5. Arendt, H: *What is Authority?* In Baehr, P (2000) *The Portable Hannah Arendt*: Penguin, p.462.

6. Holbecke, L (1999) *Aligning Human Resources and Business Strategy*: Butterworth, p.72.

7. Held, D (1987) *Models of Democracy*: Polity Press, p.30.

8. Brogue, R (2007) *The Law of God*: University of Chicago Press, p.60.

CHAPTER 12 - Beyond the God of Toleration: the Christian Contribution

1. Wilberforce, S (1866) *Charge to the Diocese of Oxford 1860*: Parker, p.66.

2. Berlin, I (1996) *The Sense of Reality*: Pimlico, p.184.

3. Padwick, C (1929) *Temple Gairdner of Cairo*: SPCK, p.149.

4. Turner, FM (1974) *Rainfall, Plagues and the Prince of Wales: Journal of British Studies* vol XII, pp.46-65.

5. Maurice, FD (1869) *Social Morality*: Macmillan.

6. Durkheim, E (1965) *The Elementary Forms of the Religious Life*: Free Press.
   Berger, P (1979) *The Heretical Imperative: Contemporary Possibilities of Religious Affirmation*: Doubleday.
   Bellah, R (1970) *Beyond Belief: Essays on Religion in a Post-Traditional World*: Harper and Row.
   Parsons, T (1966) *Religion in a Modern Pluralistic Society* in *Review of Religious Research* 7, pp.125-146.

7. Andreski, S (1983) *Max Weber*: George Allen Unwin, p.135.

8. Stephens, R (2008) *The Fire Spreads*: Harvard University Press.

9. Illingworth, JR (1895) *Personality Divine and Human*: Macmillan

10. Ramachandra, V (2008) *Subverting Global Myths*: SPCK.
    Boeve, L (2007) *God Interrupts History*: Continuum.

11. Ratzinger, J (2004) *Values in a Time of Upheaval*: Crossroads.